BLOGGING

FOR BEGINNERS

*The Ultimate Beginner's Guide to Make
a Living from Blogging in 1 Hour a Day*

BRIAN WOOD

TABLE OF CONTENTS

CHAPTER ONE

Introduction to Blogging

The first thing that comes to mind when blogging is mentioned is the definition of the term blog. Many people have interacted with blogs without knowing what they are. So, there goes the first concern, what is a blog?

There are many ways in which we can look at the word. First of all, the term blog is a shortened version of a weblog. This term is used to describe websites that have ongoing records of information. This term can also be viewed as an electronic diary on the web, which has comments and links to specific articles or websites. The links are, in most cases, presented as a list of entries in reverse sequential order. Blogs can sometimes be personal and focus on a specific subject or line of information. At times blogs can be political, or something of that sort, and delve into a broader scope of information concerning various topics.

Many blogs are mostly focused on a single topic. For instance, there are ones that are solely about web design and development, sports updates and news, or technology and smart devices. Some are more wide-ranging, presenting various links to other websites with a wide range of information. In other cases, you will come across blogs that are mostly designed like personal journals with the owner's (author's) thoughts about life and everything that happens daily around them.

In general, blogs do share some common aspects, although there are some exceptions here and there. Some features that you will come across in almost every blog are:

- Feeds and pop-ups such as RRS or RDF files.

- Blogrolls, which are links that lead readers to other sites with additional information.

- A comment section after every article for readers to share their thoughts about the publications.

- A home page, which the main content area that has articles and publications. New ones are always on top and organized into categories.

- An archive of older publications.

Some blogs come with extra features, while some may not have the features mentioned above at all.

What is a Blogger?

A person who owns the blog and runs or maintains it is called the blogger. He/she is usually the one who posts articles, publications, news updates, cases, reviews, and any other information worth sharing. All the posted information is called blogposts.

Blog Content

Content is the entry on all websites. For instance, a school website will have information about their curriculum, the institution, and all relevant news concerning learning and programs. A news site will have the latest news updates and archives of the previous report. A personal blog will contain opinions, observations, or case studies. A retail website will have a list of products and their prices, etc. The bottom line is, there must be some updates or information on those sites for people to find a reason to visit them.

In the same manner, a blog must have some content; and that comes in the form of articles posted by the author (blog posts or entries). There are some blogs with multiple authors, and some even have an allowance for guest authors to make their contributions. In typical fashion, these authors write their articles in a web-based interface, which is inbuilt in the blogging system. In some cases, authors may write their articles offline and post them later on their blogs. Such a feature is called the stand-alone blog client software.

Comments

For an interactive session on the websites, the blog comes with a feature that allows visitors to leave their comments, tips, and views at the end of every article posted. This feature enables the sharing of ideas and thoughts about the blogpost.

Almost every blog has this feature to enable people to share their opinions about the articles posted. Some blogs also have nifty ways that other authors may use to comment on articles without visiting the blog. These features are called trackbacks or pingbacks, and they ensure that bloggers communicate among themselves easily through their websites.

The Difference Between a Blog and a Content Management System (CMS)

CMS is software that provides a way of managing a website, and a lot of blogging software programs are categorized as types of content management systems (CMS). The CMS offers features that can be used to set up, manage, and maintain a blog. At the same time, they make Internet publications simple, just like writing articles with titles and having them arranged according to their categories and specifications. A primary CMS blogging tool should provide a simple interface that enables authors to write and post their content. At the same time, it takes care of the other logistics, such as making the posts more presentable and readily available to the public. In simple terms, the blogger is given ample time to concentrate on their topics of discussion while the tool helps in the entire management of the site. However, some CMS are very complicated with sophisticated features.

An excellent example of such a blogging tool is WordPress that comes with a range of features. The device has an Administration Screen that allows bloggers to set up options that control how their websites behave and present their blog. Through the feature, an author can easily compose an article and publish it online with a simple push of a button. WordPress goes a long way to make sure that blog posts are beautifully presented in the right fonts, and the HTML codes are generated following the standards of the website.

Terms That Bloggers Should Know

In addition to having the necessary knowledge of how blogging software works, bloggers should also understand some terms and concepts related to blogging. Here are some:

Archives

A blog is one way that a person can keep track of significant events and articles. Some blogs come with the archive feature, which is based on calendar dates. For instance, yearly archives. Some have daily files on the front page of the weblog. Archives can also be presented based on specifications and categories of articles on the site. Posts can also be archived based on their authors or in alphabetical order. There are endless possibilities when filing content. A blog becomes a personal tool for publications and presentations of ideas, views, and other relevant information because of the ability to have the content arranged and presented in a systematized fashion.

Feeds

A feed is a special function in a website that allows people visiting the site to access the new content and then post the same content on other websites. It is a way that users can keep track of the latest information posted on the site. Feeds may include RSS, RDF files, or Atom.

Syndication

As stated above, a feed is considered a machine-readable content that is published regularly on a web. Weblogs update their feeds for users to access information all the time. There are tools (feedreaders) that check specified blogs to see if there are new feeds posted or when there are any updates on the sites. If so, the tools display those updates with a link and part of the post (or the entire post). When going through the feeds, the feedreader checks if there are new items that can be downloaded for users to read, which saves them time visiting the blogs they like. All that is there for readers to do is adding links to the RSS feed of blogs that they would like to visit. The feedreader then informs the user when there are any new items posted. These feeds are called syndication feeds.

Managing Comments

As said, comments are one of the most exciting features in a blogging tool. They make the blog interactive and allow users to share their opinion once there is an update on the site. Users can also share links to your post and recommend them using trackbacks and pingbacks. We are going to discuss how you can manage and moderate comments posted on your blog. On the same line, we will see how you can handle comment spam on your weblog.

Trackbacks

Initially, they were designed and created by SixApart, the developers of the MovableType blog package.

In general, trackbacks were created to provide a better way in which there can be notifications within different sites. In simple terms, they are a way in which X can communicate to Y by telling them about something they would like on X's website. In that case, X would send a trackback ping to Y.

Let us take a better look at it using an elaborate example:

- X posts an article on their weblog.

- Y intends to post a comment on X's blog about the article and, at the same time, wants her readers (Y's) to see her opinion and get the chance also to comment, but on her site.

- Y posts her blog and sends a trackback ping to X's weblog.

- X's blog receives the trackback and put it on display as a comment to the initial post. The feedback has a link that leads to Y's post (on Y's site).

The basic idea that brought about by the setup is that more readers are introduced to the post since both followers from X and Y sites are both able to follow the link to the article. The trackback also brings some level of authenticity to the post as it comes from another weblog. However, there are no ways that a person can verify any trackback, and that might pose the risk of fake trackbacks.

In most cases, trackbacks only send a section of the article to X of what Y has to say about the item. This setup acts as a teaser to make X and his readers click the link leading to Y's site and read the full comment.

X can edit the comment of Y in his site, which also compromises the whole idea of authenticity.

Pingbacks

Pingbacks are meant to solve some challenges posed by the trackbacks. And that is the reason for the pingback documentation:

to act as a description of a trackback. Let us take a look at an elaborate example:

A writes an article on her blog. B reads the article and comments on it while creating a link to the initial report. By the use of pingbacks, the software of B will automatically notify A that there is a link created to her original post. The software of A, from her side, then includes the information on A's site. This feature will only work if both A and B have pingback enabled blogs.

The best way of looking at it is by thinking of a pingback as a remote comment, which is generally displayed on a person's blog as a link from another person's post. There is a general misconception that unlike trackbacks, they do not send content to the initial article. But that is not true because when a pingback pops, there is always an excerpt from the other blog displayed on the comment section on the original post owner's dashboard. However, there are very few themes that show such parts of the post from the pingback. For instance, if using WordPress, the default theme will not display any excerpts.

There is only one feature that differentiates pingbacks from trackbacks, and that is the technology that both use. Pingbacks use XML-RPC while trackbacks use HTTP POST. The difference is, however, useful in the sense that pingbacks cannot be targeted by spam since it has an automatic verification process. To some people, trackbacks remain the better of the two because readers of X can take a look at what Y has to say about the post and may decide if they want to read more by clicking on the link. And some may think about the verification connection between the two blogs as the feature that makes pingbacks the superior one of the two.

Using Trackbacks and Pingbacks

Comments posted on the comment section of a blog has often been criticized as lacking authority and moral standards since there is no way that they can be verified and regulated. In that sense, people get to say anything and use any language in giving their opinion about the post and may even go overboard to some irrelevant issues. That is where pingbacks and trackbacks in the equation to offer some way of verifying the blog comments.

Here is how you can enable trackbacks and pingbacks:

At the administration screen, go to the discussion setting and select the two items (pingbacks and trackbacks) found under the "default article settings."

- Attempt to notify any blogs linked to from the article.

- Allow link notifications from other blogs (pingbacks and trackbacks) on new articles.

Select the two options since selecting one may not go well with the other one. Once you have both of them enabled in your blog, all trackbacks and pingbacks from other sites will appear in the administration screen the same way other comments appear on your posts. In the case of blog pages, the two will appear depending on the theme design of your weblog.

Anytime you publish a post, a pingback will be sent automatically without any further actions (as long as they are enabled). But in the case of trackbacks, you will have to find the trackback URL in the post that you want to link to. If you are not able to find any URL, then the site you are trying to connect to may not be supporting trackbacks. But if the site does support the feature, then you will have to copy and paste the URL into the field that allows you to send trackbacks (it is usually found on the "Add New Post" screen). If the field is not available, then you can go to the screen option and select the "Send Trackback" option.

It is worth noting that selecting the send trackback option does not automatically send a trackback. It only brings you the send trackback field. Every time you post something new, the trackback is sent to the URL you have pasted in that field. O your Edit Post screen, the field will display for you the statuses of your pingbacks and trackbacks.

Moderating Comments on the Blog

Comment moderation is a feature that allows bloggers to monitor and regulate the comments posted on their articles. The same can also help in dealing with the issue of spam comments. In other words, it helps in the general regulation of the comments. For instance, you can delete some comments that are offensive and sensitive; you can approve good comments and let them appear in the comment section, and make any other decision you deem fit concerning people's comments on your blog posts.

Comment Spam

The term is used to describe comments that are deemed useless and irrelevant. The feedback may also include pingbacks and trackbacks to the blog post. These spam are always not related to the article posted and may go out of context and sometimes do not reflect the value of the post. They can have links to other websites that do not relate to the blogposts.

Spammers are always notorious in using comment spams to get higher page ranks for their websites and domains in Google to sell the domain names at better prices or to have a more top search ranking. Due to the large amount of money that is involved, they become relentless and may go as far as building automated tools to submit the spam comments rapidly to numerous blogs and websites. And for a beginner in blogging, this issue may be overwhelming.

WordPress has a solution to the nuisance created by spammers. They have generated many tools that are aimed at combating comment spams and ensure that bloggers can manage them effectively.

Pretty Permalinks

These tools are permanent URLs that are added to a person's weblog and other categories of blog posts. This URL is what other people will use to create a link to your post. The same gives you the chance to create a link of your post to email messages you share with your readers. The permalinks are permanent URLs of the articles you create to ensure that people can reference your work for an extended period. They do not change for a very long time.

The idea of "pretty" permalinks is brought by the notion that your URLs should always be visible to other people who click them. Therefore, these links should be generated in a way that makes sense without parameters that people cannot understand easily. Pretty permalinks should be hackable to allow users to modify the links that appear on their browsers to access other sections of the website. Let us take a look at an example of how a default permalink to an article may appear in default WordPress installation.

/index.php?p=423

This link does not bring the element of easy to comprehend, and many people might not know the meaning of "p" or the number 423.

In a move to make it more understandable and less complicated, a pretty permalink will come in a better structure as a link to the same article in the following way:

/archives/2003/05/23/my-cheese-sandwich/

In the permalink, it easy to understand that the numbers indicate the date of the posting and the words the title of the article. In the same manner, one can hack the URL and modify it to /archives/2003/05/. This way, you can get a list of all blog posts from May 2003, which is a pretty cool idea.

Blog by Email

Some blogging tools come with the feature that allows bloggers to send a posting directly to their blogs using an email without accessing the weblog interface. WordPress has this feature. What you have to do is link an email address to the website and send your blog contents directly site by email, and they are automatically posted and published.

Post Slugs

If your weblog has pretty permalink enabled, then the title of your article within the link generated will be the post slug. The title is usually simplified to an appropriate form that can be added to the link. For instance, if the title is "The Security of US Elections," it can be modified to "the-security-of-us-elections" in WordPress. That is the post slug, and you can change it to something like "us-elections-security," which is a shortened version.

Excerpt

An excerpt is a summary of the blog post or a section of the more extensive article. The passage can be written as a summary of the post or can be generated using the keywords and the first paragraphs of the entire article. The good thing is that you get to choose the section that appears as your excerpt.

Plugins

These are some bits or additional features that add some functions to the blog. For instance, you can have an added theme collection or fonts as plugins to the website. They can act by enhancing the default features or bringing an entirely new idea and design to the blog. WordPress has a way of enabling plugins in the Administration Screen, which will allow users to search for the plugins, install them, and activate them within the website.

Basic Blogging Tips

We all have to admit that starting a blog is not that easy, and that may put a lot of people off. Some people are lucky enough and may have an excellent start to blogging life, while some find it hard and get discouraged along the way. By the end of this book, you will have gathered enough knowledge to help you get started and continue blogging to get more visits, comments, and views. However, to offer you a tip of the iceberg, here are some tips that can make you stand out from the crowd of millions of other bloggers and become among the few that are successful in the industry. These tips are explained better and are more detailed in other parts of this book.

- Ensure that you have new posts all the time. But at the same time, you have to be cautious not to post things that are not catchy and are irrelevant.

- Chose specific genres that you would like to talk about and stick to them.

- Do not be quick to ask people to subscribe to your posts and blog. Wait until enough people are visiting your blog.

- Always ensure that your themes are as simple and as clean as possible.

- Enjoy what you are doing. I fact, it is better to go for the genres that excites you the most. That way, you will always have something to talk about.

- Comment on the blogs of other people. They might be interested in visiting back and commenting on yours too.

- Have fun as you blog. There are no explicit rules on what you post on your blog, so do not limit your ideas. Let it flow and share whatever you feel like.

Enjoy blogging!

CHAPTER TWO

The Importance of Creating a Blog

What comes to your mind when you hear the term blogging? If all you think about are the beautiful DIY projects on Pinterest or some flashy designer outfits, then you should try to catch with the pace of technology and change your perspective. A more significant portion of the blogging platform is mainly made up of fashion blogs and information about lifestyle and smart devices. However, blogging comes a medium that packs tons of marketing advantages to anyone and any industry. And that is even made better if you are looking to start a personal blog.

Be it looking for the first client or visitor to your blog to share in your thoughts and other posts, or you are a pro that is looking to broaden his/her scope, here are some reasons why blogging is essential.

- **It gives you a good workout session**

The writing part of the brain acts like a muscle that needs regular exercise and training to get better and in good shape. That idea alone has spawned millions of articles and blog posts about why people should write regularly. Some may believe that you should take some time off, which is not bad at all, but the concept here remains the same. The more you practice, the better you become.

You may be naturally talented with the skill of putting words together, but if you slump on training and practicing consistently, you may end up not getting better at what you do. And the moment your skills are not improved, you can forget about attracting many people. If you want to share your ideas and be heard by millions of people, then you should start blogging.

- **Blogging keeps creativity flowing**

When you are confined to the idea of writing to earn a living, you may end up leaning on a specific direction or type of writing that limits creativity. If you take a look at some blogs, you will notice a pattern that has three to four lines or sentences as an introduction to every article they do. Then the body comes with five to seven sections or paragraphs, and lastly, a conclusion of at most three sentences.

This pattern is most effective in marketing the service of some clients. But the formula approach that comes with it makes you feel like there is nothing new in your posts. Creating a personal blog allows you to tweak your content with the right tone, structure, and topics that you feel suit your style. This way, you can broaden your scope of how you like and become more creative in the process, unlike writing for someone's publications.

- **Blogging positions you as an expert in the field**

If you want people to take you seriously, you should start practicing putting your ideas down in writing and inviting them to share and review. You may have great ideas about interesting topics that can get you some reasonable contract offers. But if you cannot put them down in writing for people to see and evaluate, you people may not have the opportunity to know your capabilities and ability to implement the strategies that you have in your mind. In other words, your blog should reflect who you are or what you want people to know about your capabilities (but you are not restricted to that idea). If you are passionate about sports, write about the latest highlights, the rumors, scandals, and scores on and off the field and tracks. That way, someone will get to know your expertise and gauge you against others in the area, which makes you an expert in what you do.

The more post you rack up in your blog, the more authority you claim and wield as a pro in the industry. The status you will achieve will not only help in branding you but also get you paid for your work, and get paid big.

- **Blogging samples your work and thoughts**

Experts can confirm that they always get job offers because someone saw their blogs and like the tone and style in which they communicate their ideas. And that they would like the same for their products or businesses. Many bloggers land some lucrative deals by writing about something that catches the attention of employers or people who want the same services based on the samples they have seen.

When blogging, write the kind of content that would attract people you look forward to working with. If you want to attract the attention of a politician, write about election strategies and development programs and agendas that can be included in a manifesto. If it a food industry that you want to grab, talk about the trends in manufacturing minimally processed whole foods. In general, let your blog be a platform that people would like to visit to see what you have new about the topic you have chosen to dwell on. Make it a place that samples what you can offer in the real world.

This tactic will give your clients a taste of what they are subscribing to, and it may also save you the time of searching for jobs because it is a job on its own if you do it better. Talk about killing two birds with one stone.

- **Blogging gives more credibility and value to your niche**

It is undoubtedly that your opinion about things differs from those of other people within the same niche. Sharing your perspective in your unique way through a blog post adds more value to the ongoing conversation that gives you an edge over your competitors, especially when you look at things through a different lens.

Look at this example. Up to 75% of people prefer the initial idea. Giving it a better tweak raises that number to almost 80%. And if your version of the story stands out, you get the figures going up compared to other people with the same boring version. The value that you give your post will attract more readers while at the same time retaining the initial clients when there is something new. And that is how creating a blog can add value to your niche.

Blogging is not always about sharing the prevailing ideas on the internet. You can create your exciting topics and generate content that would attract more people to your site. And remember, the more people you have following your content, the more bucks you add to your account.

Make that first step, and you are guaranteed that you will never think about hunting for any other job. And the better and most impressive of it all, you work on your couch, sipping your favorite drink and not worrying about what your boss will think about it: you are the boss.

CHAPTER THREE

Choosing the Right Blogging Platform

At this point, you are looking to start your blog, but finding the right blogging platform is something that poses a challenge. There are many platforms out there, and getting to figure out the right one might be a little tricky. So how do you find out the one that will suit your specific need? Here, you have the opportunity of going through the most common platforms and evaluate the one that would be right for you. By the end of the chapter, you will have gone through some of the best and have essential tips that would guide your selection. To make the work even more comfortable, there are recommendations about the right site, according to its performance, as rated by other users.

Below are some most popular blogging platforms that are compared and discussed in this chapter.

- WordPress.org

- WordPress.com

- Tumblr

- Wix

- Ghost

- Squarespace

- Medium

- Constant Contact Website Builder

- Blogger

- Gator

What to Look for While Selecting the Right Blogging Platform

The list is broad, and some are not included here. But before going for any, it is essential to have in mind the things that you should look for when choosing a blogging platform. The first thing that you need as a beginner is a platform that has no complicated setup procedures. That is to mean, it must be easy for you to create your blog with low learning curves and no coding skills at all.

The second thing to keep on mind is the type of blog you want to create at the moment and in the future too. The reasoning behind this idea is that your blog will require additional changes and more features as it grows with time, and your audience base becomes bigger. In that case, you will have to go for a blogging platform that offers flexible options that can accommodate such changes. Going for the wrong platform may make it difficult for you to make the necessary transition in the future.

And the last bit is that you must have smart strategies to make some money off your blogging. Even if it does not cross your mind at the moment, you will have to think about it later on as your blog grows. So have in mind a platform that would enable you to make good money from your blogging activities.

With all these considerations, let us take a look at some platforms and compare them to see the right fit for you as a beginner.

WordPress.org

WordPress.org is currently the largest and most popular blogging platform around the globe. It hosts and supports more than 30% of all websites on the internet, having started in 2003. It is an open-source, free blogging platform that gives users the chance to create their websites and start blogging right away. Before creating an account, you will be required to sign up with WordPress hosting provider since it is a self-hosting platform. It is the best option if you are looking to have full control over your site in the long run.

It is worth noting that there are WordPress.org and WordPress.com, and the two should not be confused. Later on, we will look at WordPress.com.

Advantages

- WordPress.org gives users full control over the site and every aspect that come with it.

- The platform is designed to allow users to grow their blogs by adding more features, such as forums, online stores, and many more. This makes it the best blogging platform that you can use to earn some decent money.

- The site comes with many themes for users to apply to their blogs. You can choose items that make your website attractive and appealing to your clients. The best part is that you can also add some third-party themes as plugins.

- If you go for wordpress.org, you will have instant access to more than 50,000 plugins that are designed to make the website easier to manage. Some plugins also allow you to add media to your blogs, such as videos.

- The site is extremely friendly to search engines. For instance, you can create URLs that are compatible with an SEO, categories, and even tags for the blog contents that you create and publish on your site. Additionally, there are SEO plugins that you can add to the weblog as features.

Disadvantages

- The process of managing a weblog comes with a particular need for some basic knowledge.

- Managing your backups and security is your task because you have full control of the blog.

Pricing

The software is free, but to start any site, you will need a domain name and some hosting fees. For the domain name, you will be charged around $14.99 per year and $7.99 per month for hosting services. For a beginner, you can use Bluehost at a monthly fee of $2.75. Bluehost is an officially recommended hosting provider for WordPress that new users can go to get a 60% discount on hosting and a free domain name.

Constant Contact Website Builder

This platform is powered by Artificial Intelligence (AI) and allows users to create free blogs, online stores, and business websites in a matter of minutes. To get started, you are required to go through the extensive collection of templates and customize the site how you would like it to look. You are then to design other aspects of the website by dragging and dropping the interface. In addition to that, the site software gives you access to additional features like the logo maker, professional stock photo library that has more than 550,000 images, among other amazing features.

Advantages

- You can drag and drop the website interface quickly as it requires no technical skills.

- The setup process is easy and takes less time since the software hosts the website for users.

- Some free plans would require users to try out some features like building online stores before they can decide to purchase the feature.

- The software comes with a free domain name and an SSL certificate for all paid plans.

Disadvantages

- The scope that the developer operates in is small, and therefore there is no provision for most plugins compared to WordPress.org.

- There is limited access to third-party platforms, which may limit the way you share your ideas.

- The process of exporting the website to another platform is very complicated and challenging.

Pricing

This is one of the most generous blogging platforms that offer a free plan that allows bloggers to set up websites and even online stores.

To upgrade the starter plan, you will have to pay a monthly fee of $10, which will give you a free customized domain name, SSL certificate, and additional features such support for the platform on the phone. Compared to other website builders, phone support is a big plus due to its efficiency.

For the business plan and other eCommerce features, you will pay a monthly subscription of $20. For starters and small businesses that do not want to use WordPress for blogging, then Constant Contact offers a good alternative, especially with the prices.

Gator (HostGator)

This is a website builder and blogging platform that was developed by HostGator. The company also used to host WPBeginner websites. It offers a feature that allows users to drag and drop interface when creating any given type of websites, blogs, online stores, and any other business site. Gator builder and HostGator are different in the sense that HostGator can be used to host WordPress blogs (in other words, HostGator is a hosting service provider).

On the other hand, Gator offers the non-WordPress blogging platform solutions all in one software.

Advantages

- The website builder interface is easy to drag and drop, thus making it easy to design the website as you want.

- There are no technical skills required for the setup phase.

- All the backups, securities, and the entire performance of the blog are handled by the provider to free you some time to focus on other aspects like creating better blog posts.

- There are free domains and SSL certificates for the plans you pay for.

- There are possibilities of adding an online store to your blog, and that is just a click away.

Disadvantages

- The site does not offer any free account. However, you are given a 45-day money-back warranty.

- The features that support eCommerce are only restricted to plans that attract higher payments.

- The number of apps and extensions are minimal.

Pricing

For the WPBeginner, the users are given a 55% discount on all the plans. The starter plan goes for a monthly fee of $3.46, and it has all the features that a user needs to set up a bog successfully. It also comes with a free domain and SSL certificate.

WordPress.com

This blog hosting service is offered by Automattic, which also created WordPress.org. The company is a co-founder of Matt Mullenweg.

The site offers web hosting services for free. However, the services are limited to the basics. If you want additional features and options such as a customized domain name, extra storage space, and other premium services, then you will have to pay for them. The platform was established in 2005 to enlarge the audience of WordPress. This is among the best platforms for bloggers who do not want the extra features offered by WordPress.org, such as self-hosting.

Advantages

- There is no setup required to have your blog running.

- The site is easily manageable, and its use is also not complicated.

- If you are okay with the subdomain it offers, then it comes ultimately free of charge. In that case, the free website name will be something like this: https://name.wordpress.com.

Disadvantages

- The site provides minimal options that you can use to expand and extend your blog. For instance, there is no room for plugins and other third-party features that can be used to customize the site.

- If you decide to use this platform for your blogging activities, then forget about running advertisements. In that place, WordPress will run their adverts on your website instead.

- The account can be suspended at any given time if you go against the terms and conditions of use. That means you do not own the site.

Pricing

WordPress.com offers a basic account free of any charges. In that case, the account will have WordPress adverts and brandings.

There is an option to upgrade to a personal plan, and it comes at $4 per month (it is billed per year). This feature will ensure that the WordPress logo does not appear on your site, and all WordPress ads are removed. Your domain name is also customized to something like www.name.com.

There are even more features and design tools offered for a plan that goes for $8 per month but is billed annually.

Always beware of the tool you go for. Some people often mistake WordPress.com for WordPress.org and end up getting services that they never wanted or lacking the features they needed. You don't have to start your blog and switch later when you notice the difference.

Blogger

This is one of the oldest blogging platforms. It was initially developed by Pyra Labs in 1999 but was later bought by Google in 2003 and redesigned to be given a look and features it has today. It is a free blogging service that does not require any technical knowhow to get started.

It easy to get started, as all that is required is a google account to create a free blog.

Advantages

- It is free to create a blog on blogger.

- Managing the blog is easy, as it requires no technical skill.

- The platform is owned by Google, which gives it robust security and a decisive advantage over the other ones.

Disadvantages

- Google has a terrible history of abandoning their projects without prior warning to the user. An example is Feedburner. With this in mind, your account can be suspended or canceled at any given time, should you go against the user policies or if Google decides to cancel the service altogether.

- There are limited options to design your blog, and few templates are offered. Additionally, the third-party features available for Blogger are often of low quality.

- Frequent updates and new features are minimal.

- There are no options to add extra features, even when your blog grows. In general, Blogger offers essential blogging tools without upgrades.

In most cases, bloggers often start by using Blogger because it offers free services. But as their blogs grow and their audience becomes more significant, they switch to WordPress to access more features and more control of their sites.

Pricing

The services offered by Blogger are free, and it comes with a subdomain like https://name.blogspot.com. In case you want a customized domain name, you can purchase them from a third-party domain registrar.

Tumblr

This platform is a bit different from the other platforms in some ways. I fact, it is a microblogging platform. Tumblr offers some unique services like additional social networking features that allow users to follow other blogs and reblog. It also comes with built-in sharing features and tools, among others.

Advantages

- The site is free if you want to use its subdomain that comes in the form of https://name.tumblr.com. There is also an option to go for a premium domain name, which is charged.

- The setup process is easy and manageable to many.

- The platform comes with a unique feature that incorporates social media components.

- Since the site is mainly a microblogging tool, logging videos, GIFs, audio, and any other media is easy and fast.

Disadvantages

- The site has limited features and does not allow users to expand and extend their blogs as they grow and have a more significant audience.

- The many themes that are available for download on Tumblr do not have additional features.

- The process of backing up a Tumblr blog is very complex and challenging. The same applies to move it to another blogging platform.

Pricing

There are no charges when using the Tumblr primary subdomain. In case you want a custom domain name, then you will have to pay for it from a third party. There are also third-party themes that you can buy and use to customize your blog.

Medium

Medium has grown over the years since 2012 and is preferred by many bloggers, writers, and other experts. Using Medium is pretty easy, and it comes with limited social networking features.

This site works more like a social media platform in the sense that it allows users to create an account and start posting their articles straight away. After signing up, users are given a profile address that takes this form: https://medium.com/@name. In contrast to other platforms, users cannot use their custom domain names on Medium.

Advantages

- You do not need to have any coding skills to set up and use Medium. The entire process is easy and onetime.

- The medium allows a blogger to reach out and share with the existing community of people with similar interests.

- Instead of taking the time to design and customize your site, you are allowed enough time to focus on creating your blog content.

Disadvantages

- On Medium, you do not own the audience, which means that the moment you lose or close your account, you also lose the followers you had on the platform.

- There are minimal features in the sense that you cannot design your account according to your preferences.

- The medium does not let you have a custom domain name. All you have is the profile page name, like in the case of Facebook.

- Making money from personal ads is not possible on medium.

Pricing

Medium services are free to use.

For someone looking to make money off your blogging activities, Medium is one place you do not want to create your blog. Avoid this by all means possible.

Squarespace

Using simplified drag and drop tools, users can create beautiful websites on Squarespace. The site is mainly meant for small businesses and starters looking for an easy way to get a right online presence. For a beginner, it offers one of the best solutions on matters, creating a blog. The site is steadily growing and supports millions of websites on the internet.

Advantages

- For beginners without technical skills on matters technology, Squarespace is the place to start your blog.

- The site comes with beautifully designed templates to customize your website.

- The site also offers separate customized domain names with SSL/HTTPs as well as online stores.

Disadvantages

- The proprietary platform of Squarespace has limited inbuilt features.

- Adding more features is limited to some few services and tools.

Pricing

The site offers different pricing plans for its websites and online stores.

For a personal website, you will have to part ways with $16 every month. In case you decide to pay for the entire year in advance, you have to pay $12 monthly. If you want to have a business plan, you will pay $26 per month or may have to pay $18 per month if it is billed yearly.

For the online stores, the platform offers a plan that ranges for $26 to $40 per month, depending on the services you want.

Due to the expensive pricing, you may want to reconsider using this platform to host your blog.

Wix

This a hosted platform that allows users to build their websites. It was initially founded in 2006, and it offers the possibility to design creative and beautiful sites without any coding skills. To add a blog to the Wix website, you have to use the Wix blog app. It currently supports more than 110 million websites on the internet and allows users to build their sites by simply dragging and dropping interface.

Advantages

- There are many templates and third-party apps that users can utilize to customize the appearance of their sites.

- You only need to drag and drop the interface to create a weblog. There are no coding skills required to make this happen.

- The process of setting up is easy and faster.

Disadvantages

- The account that is not charged has limited features and comes with Wix adverts and brandings.

- Third-party apps are limited, especially if they offered free of charge.

- There are options for changing a template once applied. This means you are stuck with one design.

- The blog features are minimal compared to all other sites listed above.

- Ecommerce features can only be accessed if you pay for the plan. And even in that case, the features are still limited.

Pricing

The essential services are provided free of charge. In this case, you will be given a free subdomain name that takes the following form: https://name.wixsite.com/name. You can also have a customized domain name that comes at $4.50 per month. If you opt for the premium plans, you will have to pay a monthly fee that ranges from $8.50 to $24.50.

Ghost

This is the most straightforward blogging platform that concentrates solely on writing blog content. The company was founded in 2013 and is up to date available for users who want a platform that can host their websites. It also comes as software that can be installed and self-hosted.

Advantages

- The site is solely focused on blogging and creating blog content.

- The user interface is spotless and intuitive.

- The site is so fast because it is written in JavaScript.

- For the hosted version, you will not require setting up the interface.

Disadvantages

- The process of customizing the site with other apps is very complicated.

- Options are minimal since the interface is super simplified.

- Themes are limited; hence changing the appearance of the site is not easy.

- In case you install the software yourself, you will have problems setting it up.

Pricing

If you go for the self-hosted version, you will have to pay an annual subscription of $14.99 for the custom domain name and a monthly fee of $7.99 for hosting services.

The hosted version prices start from $29 per month (the page view limit for this plan is 100,000).

The Best Blogging Platforms

Of all the platforms discussed in this chapter, WordPress.org offers the best services and features for bloggers looking to earn a living off their contents compared to the rest of the web hosting and building tools. WordPress.org is not only sturdy and easy to use but also offers affordable rates and is flexible to changes whenever you want to make any.

The other blogging platform that offers excellent services for beginners is the Constant Contact Website Builder. The free AI-powered drag and drop tool makes it easy to set up and is suitable for any type of website, not only a blog.

CHAPTER FOUR

The Steps of Creating Blogs

Back in the days, creating a blog was so complicated and was an idea left for the few tech-savvy who could navigate the complex set up procedures. The situation as it is in the current era is different. It is much easier for anyone to start a blog practically, and the case is much proven by the thousands of blogs cropping up on the internet daily.

But how can you create a blog? For a beginner, there are some things that you must get right for your blog to be successful. For instance, there are tools that you need to have things off the ground. People looking to start blogs often ask many questions about the right boxes to click and the vital tips to get them started. This chapter tries to cover the basics of how someone can create a blog from scratch. There is also an example of getting started using Bluehost, which is among the most commonly used web hosting tools.

In a nutshell, the chapter will be looking at two steps:

- Step by step mini-course on starting a personal blog

- Practical steps for getting started on Bluehost

Step by step mini-course on starting an own blog

Many online and offline sources have a basic knowledge of how you can start a blog quick. However, there are some misconceptions as some may be lengthy, while some try to simplify the process to look more natural than it is in real sense. Here, you have the process broken down into five simple steps:

Step One: Decide on your Niche

The first question you need to ask yourself is what you want to write about. Choosing a blogging niche to target may require that you do some self-reflection and introspection. The best idea is going for an area that you are well versed in, and if not, then you must be passionate about the topics you want to cover. The moment you opt to blog to share some knowledge with other people, you must have more than the basics of the subject you have chosen to dwell on. The challenge of blogging about something that you are passionate about is that you might lose interest in the long run, and may even quit blogging altogether.

Some blogger has opted to take the notion about blogs being "online diaries" literally and end up turning their weblogs into personal spaces where they rant and rave about mundane things. In that sense, they talk about everything under the sun. In most cases, such blogs end up becoming unsuccessful. So the first thing you need to do is narrowing down to a particular topic to give your blog a sense of focus and direction.

Go for a niche that you have more interest in because it will inspire you to keep going, and you will enjoy what you are doing. Be it technology and smart devices, cooking and everything culinary, or event photography, pick what makes you enjoy your work. That would be your starting point.

Step Two: Decide On the Blogging Platform You Want to Use

For a successful blog, you must get the blogging platform and the web hosting service right.

The Blogging Platform

This tool goes a long way to differentiate an official website from a blog. The medium (software) is what turns a site into a useful weblog. As discussed in the previous chapter, a blogging platform has features that help in the management of the blog page in terms of posting new articles, general management, and search engine optimization, among other essential services.

For the right blogging platform, you should consider the following:

The cost: make sure that the money you spend is worth your while. But the good news is that most of these platforms are free unless you want additional features or premium services.

The simplicity of the interface: for a beginner, it is advisable to go for platforms that have customization options. You will not want to run into complex processes that are not manageable for someone without technical coding skills.

Appearance: you may have an idea about how you want your blog to look and feel. Some platforms can make your blog have a professional or personal appeal with the customization options at the offer. Go for a medium that would give you the right themes and designs that suit your preference.

Security and reliability: some blogging platforms do not offer effective backup options and are more prone to security threats. Go for one that provides proper security features to ensure that your contents are safe.

Availability of technical support: no matter how knowledgeable you are, some snags need support from the service providers and ones that you will need help to navigate. It would be better if your platform offers technical assistance in time.

The Webhosting Service

A web hosting service provider is a software that offers you space to conduct your blogging business on their server. They will make your blog accessible on the internet. In simple terms, they give you space on the worldwide web to parade what you have. Bluehost is one of the most affordable and effective web hosting software programs for beginners. You can also choose to use some free alternatives, but they will not allow you to have a custom domain name.

If you want to make blogging your primary source of income, then it is better to go for self-hosting instead of the free hosting options. Paying for premium services gives you the ability to have your preferred domain name and full control of your weblog. All the hosting software has different rates, features, and additional options. Here are the things to consider when choosing the right one for your blog.

Amount of web space provided: your blog is sure to grow at some point. That means that you should have a provider that can grow with you. The webspace on offer should more than enough to extend your weblog and activities.

The cost of hosting: you are willing to pay for the hosting services, and that is okay, but how much are you ready to part ways with? It is crucial to compare fees and decide on the one that will not become difficult to manage. Your willingness to pay must be in line with your capacity to do so.

Availability of customization tools: the right web hosting platform should come with a degree of control for the user. You should go for the type that offers better customization tools, features, and security aspects that will suit your preference. Compare all the available tools before you pick one.

Other vital aspects are security measures, uptime, and the speed of the server. You do not want to run into many breakdowns when you are just getting started. That would take your time and might cost you in the end. If the blog does not load fast enough, your audience may find alternatives, so the speed is equally essential.

Step Three: Design and Tweak the Blog How You Want it to Look

After choosing a blogging platform and the right web host, the next step would be to create the blog. There are practical steps of setting up a blog with Bluehost at the end of the chapter. It should guide you into getting things right. The first thing would be to register your account, then follow these tips:

- **Choose your domain name**

The domain name may be the URL or a string of words that users need to type in the address bar to get a view of your blog. The name is also an identity of the blog, which should trigger some brainstorming to get it right and catchy. You can go for a name that reflects what you have to offer. Alternatively, you can have a domain name generator do the work for you. For instance, Namemesh is a domain name generator that requires you to only feed in your ideas and keywords; then, you will have some great combinations that you can buy for a domain name.

Here are some issues that you should consider when picking a domain name:

Your pick should be simple and memorable. Some people tend to go for complicated domain names that are difficult to type in the address bar when browsing. Pick one that your users will not have a hard time searching for when trying to find your blog.

A good trick would be going for short names that are catchy and easy to spell out. That does not mean that you go something so obvious and too simple. You can to join two words like on Facebook, play with words as seen on Pinterest, or come up with something new altogether (Etsy).

The second aspect is ensuring that your domain name and the niche you have chosen to work on are identifiable and relate well to each other. If you decide to go keywords, ensure that they have an accessible register with your audience in the sense that they will immediately get an idea of what to expect in your posts by simply reading the domain name.

The extension you use for the domain name should also be specific and relevant. Some of the most used extensions are .com, .info, .net, and .biz.

- **Design the look and feel of your blog.**

At this point, you will want to give your blog the best appearance by designing it to look how you want. Here are some tips:

Choose a good theme: go through the customization tools and all available design options and templates. If the blogging platform offers a range of themes like in WordPress, then you have half of the work done for you. All you have left is choosing the right theme and applying it to your interface. Tweak the features to get the right look for your blog. Your weblog must be catchy and attractive. On the other hand, it is also crucial to go for simple themes that would not make your site too colorful for no god reason.

If you are well versed with coding knowledge, then tweaking your blog should not be an issue. But if you have no technical skills, you can also get going by applying the StudioPress theme that is based on the Genesis framework found in WordPress. Genesis offers some professional help that helps in designing weblogs.

Tweak the blog: the fun part of setting up a blog is getting to tweak things the way you like. After choosing the theme, you will have to modify the theme and other aspects that would give your weblog a good look. You can play with the fonts, color, images, and any other feature that would influence the appearance of the site. Blogging platforms with customization options make it easy to have all these done.

Choose the right plugins to add: there are many plugins available for use, and you may be tempted to go around picking anything that you can lay your hands on. However, you should only choose what is right and necessary for you. The best plugins for a beginner should be the share-button ones that allow you to link your weblog to social media platforms, the calendar plugins, the ones that filter comments and spam, and database and backup options among others.

Step 4: Make the Blog Live!

You have gone through the basics steps of setting up your blog. Now it is time to get things running: to launch the blog. You can set a specific day for the event then share then good news with some friends and family. Letting the people close to you know that you are about to launch a blog should be the first step in marketing your brand.

Step 5: Post Great Content

Everything is all set, and it is that time you fill the blog with exciting headlines and engaging content that will get your visitors glued to your blog and coming back for more. And as they say, good content is okay, but great content is everything.

Your content should be creatively done and great to read. Additionally, you must ensure that whatever appears on the blog is always compelling, relevant, and add more value to the lives of your readers. The content should either instill some knowledge, update on new things, or solve existing problems.

The presentation of the content also matters a lot. If possible, add some media to the content such as images, videos, or GIFs that go well with what you have written. The media add some value to the content and makes it more appealing to the visitors.

Your contents should also be updated regularly and in good time to ensure that your visitors do not wait long for the next issue. You have this done by scheduling your updates or linking your blog to your email to enable you to publish directly from the email. Always remember that an active blog will get you more clients and add extra cash to your pocket. In contrast, an inactive one will not attract many people.

- **Practical steps for getting started on Bluehost**

Bluehost stands out as one of the most used and trusted web hosting providers. The platform was launched in 2003 and has grown over the years to become one of the best in the industry. For beginners, Bluehost is the best site to get started. The rates offered for the services are pretty low, and the setup procedure is easy, simple, and requires no technical expertise to navigate through. And the most impressive thing is that it partners with WordPress to provide some impressive features.

For $3.95 per month, you can have Bluehost to host your weblog plus a free custom domain name, website builder, and WordPress installation with just a simple click. The provider also offers technical support around the clock through chats, email, or phone. Here are some steps that will get you started in just five minutes:

- **Create an account with Bluehost**

Go to the Bluehost site and click on the "get started now" button. Proceed by choosing a plan that you feel will suit your needs. There are three plans you can choose from: BASIC, PLUS, and PRO. For a beginner, BASIC would be a great plan. You can upgrade to PLUS or PRO later on as your blog grows and requires additional features.

For the BASIC plan, you will have to pay $3.95 per month at the package comes with a 50GB storage space for a single website, a custom domain name, and five email accounts, each having 100MB storage space.

After that procedure, you will have to provide a domain name. In case you already have one, you can just sign up with it. There is another option box that gives you the chance to fill in a new domain name. If the domain you requested is available, you have directions to lead you to the next step. Additionally, you get to choose an extension of your preference.

- **Fill in the forms that are presented to you**

These are some of the information that you will be requested to provide:

Account info: this includes all personal information, such as your address and contact details.

Package information: here, you will have to fill the duration of the plan you want and the price. It is about choosing an account plan for your blog. You can also add some add-ons like SiteLock security, privacy protection, constant contact, among other options. All the options will go for will indicate its corresponding charge. The best thing to do for a beginner is ignoring all the possibilities. Just uncheck all the boxes until that time when your blog has grown and needs these features.

Next, you will go to the billing option, which requires you to choose a payment option you prefer.

- **Agree to terms and conditions**

Confirm that you agree to the terms and conditions of Bluehost. It is essential to read the terms and understand what you are signing up for. After going through the terms, click submit.

The next page will give you additional options for upgrades and other features to buy. It is better to skip them for the time being by clicking on Complete. And there you go, you have successfully signed up to a Bluehost account.

You will receive a confirmation email via the email you used to sign up. Confirm if you can access the account successfully. After that, create a password for the account. Remember to follow the parameters that make your password secure enough.

- **Log in to the account**

Using the password, you have created a log into the account. You will see a welcome message popping up, followed by two options. You can either choose to get started on your own or let the Bluehost team do it for you. But it is better to do it yourself. That way, you get to familiarize yourself with the dashboard and learn some essentials in the process.

- **Install WordPress**

Bluehost has a one-click step for installing WordPress, which makes it easy for users even without some technical skills.

The InstallWordPress icon is found at the bottom of the home screen. Once you click it, you will be led to the page with INSTALL. Click it.

The next step is adding the name of your blog, your username, and the password for your WordPress after clicking the Show advanced options button. Lastly, click the option indicated INSTALL NOW and wait until the installation process is complete.

MOJO marketplace will send you an email with the URL of your site, the URL of your WordPress admin login, and the username. You can keep this email for reference.

Login to the WordPress account to familiarize yourself with the dashboard, learn the basics, and start designing your blog.

Select the themes you would want to apply to your blog under the appearance option and add them to your WordPress blog. You can customize the theme to have a better look according to your preference. Additionally, you can upload some plugins to make the blog look more appealing. Once everything is set, and you are satisfied with the look that you have given your blog, you can save the changes and activate the site. You are now free to start posting your articles and keeping your weblog active.

Creating a Blog is Easy!

Additional Resources and Useful Tools for Blogging

Some blogging platforms like WordPress provide some, if not all, the tools that are needed to start a blog. That should give you a good head start. The blogging platform and the web hosting service provider are the essential tools that you require to get started. However, some other tools and resources can make the entire process easy and enjoyable. They enhance the appearance and performance of the blog. Here are some:

Google Analytics: to become a successful blogger, you must have this tool. Utilizing the power of Google Analytics can help you enhance the performance of your blog.

Graphic design tools: you will need these tools to design your logos, images, and any other visual element that you may want to add alongside your posts.

Tools that manage your social media platforms: if you want to incorporate your social media platforms to the blog, you will have some tools that manage those aspects for you.

Content management tools: it is essential to have tools that can manage your content and plan for your publishing unless you write everything by hand. Even so, you will eventually grow, and you will need a scheduled posting to ensure that your content is always posted in good time.

Extra Tips on Starting a Blog

The first thing to keep in mind is that your blog will grow at some point in time, and you will have to upgrade. And in the process of blogging, you will make mistakes. It happens to pros. What you have to do is count on the errors. Ensure that you can identify where you went wrong. Catch the mistakes and learn from them so that you will not repeat the same in the future.

It is not sinful to ask questions or seek help from other bloggers. Comment on their posts and share ideas. Whenever you are stuck, you can always turn to the many online solutions or call a friend for help.

CHAPTER FIVE

Finding the Right Idea

You are at a point where your blog is fully set up and ready to go. The next thing coming to the mind is getting the right ideas of what to write about and make the blog active and appealing. It might not be easy to get the best intentions, especially for beginners. However, some tips can help you navigate this challenge. Below are a few steps that can get you going and give you the best ideas for your blog posts:

- **Solicit feedback from other people**

You may want to know the hottest areas to write about by asking people what they have in mind. It might be in the form of what they want to learn about or the challenges they look forward to solving. There must be a good connection between your ideas and the need of the people. For instance, this book can be used as a good example. It was inspired by the need to address this area as many people want to find a way of working at home and making good money off it.

For a new blogger, the audience may not be that huge to give you the best response to exciting areas. All the same, you can still post your inquiries on community forum sites to find out what other people are interested in. In some cases, you may not need to ask. You can just read through what most people follow. Listen to what they say on social media platforms and the kind of conversations they have going.

- **Be very active in your niche**

Being active in your niche will give you so much to write about. Additionally, you will be in a position to provide the latest updates and attract many readers. To become more active, you need to follow the most recent trends and news and participate in anything that covers the area you have decided to concentrate on.

You can also subscribe to top blogs in the field you are writing about and keep up with anything new going on in your niche and the industry at large. That would give you enough ideas to implement on your blog.

- **Utilize the power of social media in the industry**

You have to keep an eye on all social media platforms because those are the areas that most people interact with. Check what is happening on Facebook, Twitter, Instagram, and any other social network, especially the ones that people in your industry like using.

The best way of going about this is by monitoring the relevant keywords to figure out the areas of discussions and the key topics that keep their conversations going. In most cases, you will find out that the result of what you are searching for is enough to get your **blog lively.**

- **Keep a close eye on the community sites**

Be active on the community sites. And by this, you have to visit the industry category on sites like Yahoo Answers and Quora. These sites will give many clues on the topics that people want to know about, and that should be a starting point for your blog.

- **Do not limit yourself**

There are many ideas that you can have on the blog posts that you can ever imagine. You just need to expand your thinking and the way you look at things in your niche. Do not limit yourself. And by that, you should start seeing things beyond the scope you have decided to focus on. For instance, if you are writing about blogging, you can go the extra mile and talk about marketing and making money off blogging because that is an area that most bloggers want to learn. And if you decide to talk about health, you can also include diets and fitness because they make a good part of overall health and are essential for one to lead a healthy lifestyle.

- **Find what you are passionate about**

The best idea you will ever have is writing about what you know and interest you more. That is always the first advice that anybody will give you if you are looking for ideas to start a blog. But that alone is never enough, you want to make money, and if your thoughts do not attract many people, then you will not be anywhere near your goals. You have to ensure that whatever you concentrate on gets those bucks in your account.

- **Getting an idea that can be monetized**

Sometimes a basic idea is not enough to get you earning a decent salary. You need something profitable that can generate traffic to your blog and turn into a good income stream.

In general, finding the right niche for your blog is one of the essential steps in getting started, and it determines the performance of your blog against others in the industry. This area must be given considerable attention to ensure that you do not quit after some months. If you go for a niche that attracts a lot of competition, you may end up losing to the already established experts in that niche. In the same way, if you go for a smaller niche that has market appeal, then you will not make a remarkable impact to get you paid. Therefore, beginners must go somewhere in between. Below are ways that will get you a paying idea for the blog:

- **Talk about what you know and enjoy**

Starting a blog may be fun considering the processes. But there reaches a point where you need to convert that fun into some bucks. The best way of doing so is by ensuring that your posts are informative and authentic. As much as you enjoy what you are talking about, you have to ensure that you give the right information. Do not fabricate facts. People would like to be taught ways of solving their problems, be it relationship advice or some handy tips and life hacks at home. If you keep suggesting things that do not work out, they lose interest and brand you a joker and fake.

And the best way of doing fine in that respect is by going for a niche that excites you. You are moved, inspired, and motivated to learn more about what you are writing and dig deep to get all the answers that can solve the problems you want to address. So, the question is, how can you get the ideas that interest you? Here is how. Get a pen and a paper. Write some ideas that you can talk about off of the head. Chose the first five because you will find out that they are the ones that you wrote very first without even thinking hard. Research on those topics and see if they are highly demanded.

- **Conduct market research**

You have to find out if your ideas are profitable and have a market appeal and demand. That would require you to do a little market research. Here are some tips to get you started:

For instance, let us have relationship advice as an area that you would like to write about, and you want to find out if the market demand is high. The demand will be determined by the audience size as well as the level of competition in that segment.

The first thing you will do is type relationship advice on Google Trends and see if many people have searched for the topic and if it hold any appeal in the market, which is determined by the interested people about it. Google Trends will give you a graph that shows if the topic is stable, rising, or declining. That should be enough to decide whether you want to delve on the matter or should go for something else. You will not want to go topics that are on the decline because your blog may not have the right audience in the long run.

The result given will be within a range of years. You have to see if it is seasonal, or the topic has sway all the time. If the item is rising relatively, then it means that your audience will keep growing, and that will drive your traffic for many years to come. And that pays.

- **Go for a smaller niche**

The point here is that you do not want to lock horns with the most established pros in the industry. As a beginner, you will not win the competition. And that may affect your blog significantly. So you have to determine the level of competition you are about to face. To do so, you will have to search for the topic on Google search and see the number of search results you get.

The topic of giving relationship advice is so broad, and many bloggers are focusing on it. To ensure that you avoid such stiff competition, you have to go for a smaller niche. When scrolling down the search results, you see an area that has other related search terms. Pick one of the terms and see how many results you get. You should also be able to identify the number of people that are interested in that area.

Go over to AdWordsKeywordPlanner for a better analysis of the search term you have chosen. You get the number of average searches per month, which is enough to determine if it is a great idea or not.

You continue exploring other keyword ideas you will notice that some attract low competition but are very popular, and those should give you the right ideas to write about on your blog.

- **Profitability is everything**

The plan here is to earn money from the blog, and that means that whatever you are going for should be profitable enough to help you make a good income. There are ways that you can test the profitability of the topic you have chosen and to determine whether you want to continue with it or drop it for another profitable one.

The best way of doing the test is by checking if there are any brand or business advertising or the keywords you have chosen. If many people spend some money to advertise any product on AdWords that targets the keywords related to the niche that you have chosen, then that is proof enough that you have gotten it right.

That will also be an opportunity for you to earn good money by including some Ads through AdSense. Another way, which is the most profitable one, is selling affiliate products on your blog. For instance, you can join Amazon's Affiliate Program to start promoting their products. Whenever you direct a client to Amazon, and they make a purchase, you will be given a 10% commission on the product they have purchased. You can write reviews of the affiliate products and make their lists before linking them to Amazon to get paid. And that is how you can turn an idea into something that gets you paid, which is part of the reason you should start a blog.

- **Over to you**

The moment you get the right idea for your blog, ensure that you have exceptional content written down and published. This move will get you ahead of the competition by making you stand out. Consistency is also essential and should be one of your greatest assets. Always schedule your posts to get your readers something whenever they visit your blog. Accordingly, you will have to be patient. You won't attract a thousand readers overnight. You have to earn them one by one, and with the time, you can have the best audience depending on the quality of the content you give them.

- **Choosing the right topic for the blog**

First things first, getting the correct item for your blog is entirely different from finding ideas for the blog content. A topic is a foundation upon which your articles will be based on, and there might be different ideas within the same issue.

Here are some ideas about how you get the right topic to blog about:

Just like in the views, you have to be passionate about the topic of discussion. The same applies to the level of knowledge. You may like a lot of things, and the only difference, which makes a lot of sense, is the knowhow. The better you understand a topic, the most likely you will perform better at blogging about it.

You may be so much interested in technology, but how much do you know about that topic? Can you generate ideas from that subject? And for how long can you sustain the ideas? These are the kind of questions you need to ask yourself before going for a topic simply because you are interested in them.

The moment you choose a topic that you understand well, you will be able to maintain consistency for a very long time and generate creative ideas that would capture the attention of your readers. You already have some knowledge to share, and the fact that you are passionate about it will ensure that you keep looking for more options and updates about the same.

Passion and knowledge is nothing if people are not willing to spare some time and go through what you have written on your blog. You have to attract buyers and readers to like your posts. That means that you have to go for in-demand topics. What interests clients is better than what interests you as a person because you are not going to get paid for what you like. On the other hand, what readers prefer will get you paid. So the best way of going about it is ensuring that you have some feedback form your customers. Let them tell you what they would like to see in the next issue. Their response should inspire the kind of topics you dwell on. And that calls for monitoring the comment section to see what readers think about your blog posts.

Finding out the availability of information on the topics you choose is a vital part of ensuring consistency. You have to go online and figure out how much you can get about the problem from online sources. If there are a lot of resources, then you are safe. You can be assured that you will not run out of ideas to support your topic. But if the information about that topic is limited, then you would be better off getting another one. You do not want to write for one or two months straight, then find yourself stuck and unable to provide contents of the same quality.

Every situation and breakthrough you make will present more opportunities and challenges. In that sense, if you find a topic that is exhausted, then you will have to work so hard to ensure that your articles stand out from the previous ones on the same question. Likewise, if the subject has not been covered adequately, then you have to put in more effort to find information about the same.

You must have some articles ready for publishing even before you start your blog. You should write attest five posts and have them prepared before you have your blog running. That would ensure that you don't have a hard time thinking about writing when you are just getting started. And in the same line, you can keep on writing for years because you are always covered with extra content. You will not want to get stranded along the way after investing so much on your blog due to some reasons that you can avoid.

Having good content is excellent, but having great content is the best you will ever have as you start your blogging career. And all that comes with the choice of topics and ideas you want to blog about. Get it right, and you will be amazed at how many people are attracted to your site. However, if you get it wrong, you will be considering quitting along the way. What a better way than having firsthand information about the topics and preparing some articles in advance.

CHAPTER SIX

Creating Traffic

There reaches a point when you have worked so hard on the blog that you feel like a pro. And that calls for getting serious about the traffic you attract to the site. The more traffic you can create, the more you will get paid for your blogging activities. Here are some tips you can use to increase blog traffic:

- **Have a good strategy when it comes to the contents of your blog**

The first thing to do to ensure that you have more blog traffic is giving your audience quality content. You have probably come across this many times and heard other bloggers say content is king in the blogging industry. Content is not just quality alone. You have to strategize better in terms of timing your posts and the effort you put on marketing your blog.

The better blog content is one that meets a specific need of the readers. That means you know what the audience wants, what they feel, and the things they love reading about. In the current blogging era, your content will have to fall into either of these categories: Cool and funny or useful and informative. If you go for any of the segments, then you will have a good start.

If you want to get some more ideas about the kind of content people are interested in, then visit Quora and see the sort of questions people ask that relate to your topic. Another great source would be Buzzsumo. It will give an idea or two by only seeing what other people are writing about in the industry you have decided to step into. You can take it from there and make the conversation even better.

In the case of your style, you can go the extra mile by including cute videos to tell your stories, go for shocking statistics, and other colorful infographics. It is all about creating something that will move readers and stand out from the crowd of average bloggers. Create content that more people can link to and want to share with others.

- **Create content that is always green**

Ensure that a significant percentage of your blog content is evergreen. This kind of content is one that can pass the test of time. In other words, your posts should be able to stay relevant even ten years from now. For instance, if you decide to write about this years' EMAs, people will not be interested in looking at the post in two or three months. It will become irrelevant, especially when other awards come, say Oscar. However, if you go for the life of Tupac, the article will be read by generations without losing that aspect of relevance. Think about what you want to write about and evaluate if it can attract readers two or three years down the line.

- **Craft headlines that grab attention**

Giving your audience a good teaser will have them yearning to read the posts and can even wait for the Ads to finish to get a look at what you have to say. As a blogger, your headlines should be irresistible. It is what gets visitors to the blog by capturing their attention and interest. Some established bloggers will even tell you that the headline is more important than the actual post. If you have a kickass content hidden behind a shabby headline, people will not know, and that will give it a quick death.

Look at it in this manner, appearance is everything, and that is why you would not go for a wedding in your stay-home-bored pants. The same way, no one can be convinced that a lackluster headline has excellent content following.

Do not shy away from experimenting. You can have multiple headlines for a single article and see the one that attracts more people, and that should be one that you base your headline styles on. And by that, you can also have multiple forms as long as they are catchy.

- **Generate newsletters that showcase some of your great blog posts**

A big part of your content strategy should be promoting your work. That is another way that can drive more traffic to your blogs and should be one thing you are good at.

The best way of doing content promotion is by starting getting emails from your clients for the blog newsletters. Once they have trusted you enough to accept this subscription, you can send them your monthly or weekly newsletters and not forgetting to include some of the best posts you have. That action will have your clients coming back for more and also sharing what you have to offer with other people. And going by the fact that these users are already familiar with your blog, they might go the extra mile and explore more on your blog. They might start sampling the products you are promoting on the site as well.

But you must be cautious about maintaining that trust. Some people, in fact, most people, are susceptible to how their contacts are used. Do not take that as an opportunity to send anything you find to them. Nowadays, the ethical use of consumer data matters so much, and you must ensure that everything you post your readers is relevant; otherwise, they will unsubscribe from your platforms.

- **Do not fear using the keywords**

Relevant keywords and SEOs constitute a significant part of your strategy if you wish to drive traffic to your blog. Many bloggers nowadays become a bit nervous when you suggest to them anything to do with SEO. However, it is vital to keep in mind that search engine optimization can be excellent when done in the right manner. That way, you will target specific users from Google to ensure that you have them getting to your site every time they search for the particular words on the web. That is wondrous!

As much as it is recommended, SEO must come in moderation. Everything is better when done in moderation. Here is what it means:

- Should you use keywords in your context texts? The answer is yes.

- Should you stuff and saturate your blog content with keywords and search queries? No, don't even think of it.

- Should you link your post to the previous ones you have written on the same topic? Yes.

- Include links everywhere such that every paragraph has a hyperlink to another article? No.

- Conceptualize and influence your posts with keywords? Yes.

- Give more priority to keywords and search bots as opposed to user experience? No.

Google drives billions of searches a day ad; you should leverage the power of keywords and SEO to get a good pie for yourself. It is an approach that is tried and tested, and it works a great deal. But the current market has so many sites and advertisers competing for the same keywords. So how can you have the edge over the rest of the online crowd? Go for the long-tail keywords.

Why Should Bloggers go for Long-Tail Keywords?

The first thing would be to let you know what these are. Long-tail keywords are ones that have more than three keywords. They are more accessible to target and are cheaper options in terms of the PPC since the phrases always attract fewer competitions. The only sure way of getting a top SERP rank on Google is going for the long-tail keywords.

Long-tails are not only refreshing, but they are also the kind that keeps the blog lively. For instance, let us say you want a higher ranking on Google for the term health food because you are blogging about that topic. But we all how many people are using the same term, which makes it very competitive. For you to take your game to the next level, you will need to expand it to something like health food meal prep or say health food shopping basket. That way, your chances of getting a high rank will be improved drastically.

Best SEO for Bloggers: How to Find Long-Tail Keywords

The best way to brainstorm these top keywords is by checking on Google. Type any phrase on the search area and see the kind of sentences that are suggested to complete the search. These auto-completed suggestions should guide you in making the decision on which ones are mostly used and the ones that appear on top.

The nest thing should be typing the entire words that were suggested and seeing the ones that are included in the related search segment at the bottom of the search results. Get the ones that appear to be more related and are appearing in all the sections (suggested and also included in the related search section).

Go on by putting all the long-tail keywords and phrases you have gathered into the Google Keyword Planner. Find out the ones that drive the most traffic and compare them with the other ones suggested by Google. The ones with high search volumes and low competition should be the right ones for you. So every time you are creating your content, ensure that they appear on the posts (only when the article is related to the targeted keyword).

SEO WordPress Plugins that You Should Have

WordPress has a range of some cool plugins that are designed to help bloggers with SEO. These add-ins will help you set up your URL slugs in the right way and efficiently as well as guide you when crafting better descriptions, sitemaps, and any other technical bit that is associated with generating better SEO. Some of these may not come naturally to a beginner, that's why you need some help navigating these steps. The most common plugins are:

- WordPress SEO by Yoast

- All in One SEO Pack

Find the people that are interested in your ideas

To promote your blog effectively, you must strategize about the areas you want to spend most of your time. It might be okay to establish your presence on many social media platforms. But you also know that the plan comes with some challenges, and if you are not keen, you might burn out after some time. That is why it is recommended that you hunt for your flock and specialize in areas they are found.

Dip your feet and figure out where a big part of your audience is found. And also get to know the social networks that work nest for your blog. If your content is going heavy on the visuals, you will have to set your site on LinkedIn. But if your posts are more on nerd culture, then you can set your camp on the right subreddit, and you can be guaranteed that you will make it big.

They say that if you are looking for seagulls, you have to visit the shores. In the same way, if you want to drive your blog traffic, you have to establish a blog where a majority of your audience hangs out. You have to understand your readers and get them where they are.

Leverage the power of Google Analytics to drive your traffic. Google Analytics will help you understand the websites that have the most referral traffic. This way, you will find the right forums and sites that your audience likes using. Once this is done, get active and engage them in conversations. Posts some links to your weblog anytime you feel like you have their attention, and the timing is appropriate.

This is a big ask because you do not want to join a conversation and come out of it as a spam master. You have to present yourself as a valuable member of their community whenever a conversation crops up. Wait for the right moment to direct people to your site. For instance, if someone wants to know about a healthy diet, you can offer some tips, then refer them to your blog post about a healthy diet meal plan. But it would be odd to direct someone to a resource about mountain climbing tips if the conversation is about sky diving.

Learn to Move with your Crowd

- **Once you have your audience, go all in**

Make the platforms where your audience is found your focal point. You have to limit the social networks to the ones that are worth spending your time on. And that means that if you have 100 people on Twitter and none on Facebook, build your blog mostly on Twitter. That is where you have readers to impress. This approach is based on the fact that too many choices will wear you out. You do not want to overwhelm and stress your users either.

In most cases, people tend to think that more choices are better, but research shows that you may be better off with fewer options instead. But that does not mean you ignore the rest. You can keep a close eye on them, but the most focus should be on what is getting you paid.

- **Ask for what you want**

There is enough evidence to prove that users that ask other people to retweet their tweets get 73.48 retweets on average compared to 2.09 retweets for those that never ask. That means that by asking people to follow your content, they will be compelled to do so.

The same approach applies to all call-to-actions. To you, the intention will be clear, but to the visitors, the appeal will increase the likelihood to share more and follow you through the journey. But you have to offer something worth pursuing.

- **Optimize for speed and mobile use**

Nobody will spend their time on your blog waiting for your content to load. If your page is not coming up fast as they expect it to then, they will be compelled to exit and move to the next one on the Google list, which may happen to be a close competitor. So you must ensure that your site has the right speed. Do you want to see that happen? Here is how:

Google's Page Speed Insights tool helps to give the rate of your site and goes on to provide you with tips on how you can increase the speed of your website.

On the same topic, more people spend time on their mobile phones and tablets than computers. Therefore, going for mobile is a no-brainer for any blogger looking to create more traffic. You have to ensure that your blog supports mobile use and is up to snuff. You can use the following WordPress plugins to optimize your blog for mobile application:

- WPtouch Mobile Plugin

- JetPack by WordPress

- **Play calm and friendly with other bloggers**

To go all the way in online jobs, you have to exhibit good mannerisms. You have to build a good relationship with other bloggers in the same industry. Sometimes you can team up with them against a common enemy, talk of the game of thrones style. Or you may want them to help you with some ideas. Sharing ideas is all part of the blogging business.

Comment on other people's blogs and join conversations on various community platforms. You can even interview other leading bloggers or include their blogs on your top ten list as a way of supporting and appreciating their work. You can tag them to such posts to let them see how much you appreciate their work, and chances are they will also show you the same love. They will share your work on their blogs as a way of returning the favor, and that will, for sure, drive more traffic for you.

Creating links for your blog posts is good for SEO, but the moment you also link some outside sources, you let Google know that you are not a spammer. That will build a positive relationship with other people in the industry, especially the ones you are linking to.

Creating traffic may not be easy, but if you follow the right steps, you can make it a bit simple. Of course, it will take time, but it is worth your patience. Follow these steps, and you will be amazed at how your audience base grows with time.

CHAPTER SEVEN

Writing Blog Content

Y ou may be a good writer and have your blog posts win you a fan or two. But for a blogger that is not enough, you must be able to provide content that earns your legion of fans. And to do that, your content must be designed in a specific format considering the audience you are targeting and the topics you have chosen. This chapter has a step by step guide that will help you create spellbinding posts that will be adored by thousands, if not millions. Here. You offered the secrets to creating content that your audience will find irresistible.

Let us dive in.

The first thing to consider is creating a headline that grabs attention and teases your readers to open the article and read more. It is like the icing on a cake and must be designed in the best possible way. At this point, you have that in mind from the other chapters so that we will go to the second step straight away.

The Introduction Must Sell the Article in One Go

Having lured your readers to click on the item and have a look, you will not want to throw that away by having a shabby introduction. You have to keep them glued to the content by having a compelling first paragraph. Readers are always fickle. They can take a peep at the post them disappear from the blog, lickety-split!

So have to ensure that you keep them there. And the only way to continue them reading is by crafting an introduction that will have them craving for more of the post and going on and on to the end.

The first few paragraphs play a huge role in keeping the browsing commitment of your audiences. Here is how you can have the introduction blowing the minds of your readers:

- **Slightly slip into the story**

Most bloggers make a mistake with their opening style by trying to sound too academic in their introduction. You may have seen something like this one:

"According to research, 90% of people fail to achieve their goals and targets for the lack of implementation strategies..."

The research part may be an excellent statistical inclusion, but for an opening paragraph, readers will find that annoying. You can, however, turn things around by captivating. Let the readers feel like you have just read their mind. Write form the readers' perspective, try to make them feel like you understand them, and whatever is happening in their lives. In simple terms, step into their shoes.

It is also essential to start every post with a different style. Do not become predictable and machine-like in a sense that your readers will know what you will say in your opening statements for every post.

- **Create a character and get into it**

To captivate readers, you have to trigger some emotions. So every time you want to start writing a blog post, ensure that you know what you want them to feel about the article. Is it fear, anger, excitement, joy, disgust, etc.?

The next thing you will do is getting into a character to have that feeling yourself. Think as if you are addressing yourself and write as if you are letting out that emotion from the role you are playing. Shed the first tear if you want to have the same feeling about the piece of information you are sharing with them.

Map the emotional journey you want to lead your readers on and play with your emotions to infuse the feeling into your blog posts. The tip applies to the entire job, but it works even better when it felt in the introduction. That is the point where you want to trigger emotions and tease your audience to feel what you mean.

As a blogger, your feelings should seep into your words when you are writing.

- **Have your readers lured down the page**

If you want readers to stay committed to the post, you have to accelerate their experience by attracting them down the page. The more they get pulled down the page, the more faithful to the blog they get. You give them early bumps on the road, and they will be off the track in no minute. And chances are they will never come back.

The best way of luring people down the page has the following formats in your introduction:

- **Open the article with a question or a short sentence**

This is a copywriting technique that most smart bloggers use in their introduction to pull their readers in. It is more effective compared to starting a post with a long paragraph, which most readers find exhausting and tedious.

- **Slash your words in the introduction**

Does your draft introduction have 250 words? Try to make it 120, concise, and straight to the point. Summarizing the opening makes it look nice and attracts readers to have a look at the remaining paragraphs. No matter how good your content is, the moment readers realize they are about to go through a long post; they will be discouraged. Making the introduction appear smaller encourages people to go on.

It is never about the density but the quality. You must grab attention using few words.

- **Set the rhythm**

All your blog posts must have some pace and rhythm in them. The introduction should start at a higher speed as you slow things down in the other parts of the article as you continue writing. You can achieve this by:

- Using short statements. Even if it means using sentence fragments.

- Make your paragraphs shorter, something like three sentences long.

- Have your sentences woven together by delayed transitions.

- Make the sentence and paragraphs connected in a way that they lure the reader to look at the one that follows.

- Check the flow of your post by reading it out loud. Ensure that nothing is stalling and that the transitions are smooth.

Best writers are like musicians. They take their audience on a journey at the pace of their choice. There are times when the beats are fast, and at the moment, things slow down. The more you can infuse this style, the more rhythm you will give your blog contents.

- **Make the readers beg**

Get the readers asking for solutions by adding some elements of fear in the introduction. You can do this by identifying what worries your audience most. Talk about the bad things that can happen if the problems are left unsolved. Give them a peep into the worst-case scenarios. Expose their weaknesses in the right way by bringing their fears to the surface.

This tactic has two effects. The readers will feel like you understand them because you have been able to touch what they are most worried about. At the same time, they will want to know the solutions you are presenting to avoid being on the wrong side.

Everyone has fears, and it is human instincts to hide them. But that changes when they are exposed. Some sense of urgency creeps in, and all of a sudden, people want to solve their fears provided the solutions are readily available.

- **Ensure you do precisely that for your audience**

The fear to fail may be painful to take, but the moment you give them a voice, you validate them and make your audience eager to read more and have themselves freed.

- **Hint at giving solutions**

As you come to the end of the introduction, give your readers a teaser about the Promised Land. Let them know where the post is heading. If it is a solution you want to offer or tips, you are about to give them let them have that in mind as they continue reading down the page. You also have to ensure that you are not giving it all in the first paragraph that you will lack anything new in the body of the blog post. A single sentence is enough to get that excitement that will get your readers craving to read more.

And why would you do that? Here is the reason. We all get bored quickly, especially when reading is concerned. Readers must be kept on toes, and the introduction is the point where you want them to feel like this is going to be a good read. At the same time, that is not where you want to throw all the solutions, just the tip of the iceberg. Set the stage the let them follow you on the journey.

For a compelling introduction, you need to have two different drafts. Ensure that each selection has a different feeling and portrays a different emotion. Then check through the article to see which one relates well with the content of the post and has the perspective you want to take.

As a word of caution, you have to ensure that your introduction meets the user intent, no matter how excellent and eloquent your writing is. If the introduction fails to satisfy the readers, they will just hit the back button and go to the next blog.

So, What is User Intent?

This is the purpose or reason why the user searched for the article on Google. For instance, if a reader types "how to make money writing online," I Google, they are after the ideas and tips that will help them make money by writing online.

If they choose your article headline that reads "10 way to work online and get paid," and you start with a motivational Bruce Lee anecdote, chances are they will be leaving immediately without looking at the rest of the article, no matter how good the body is.

And as they leave your blog, they leave a message to Google that your site has some dumbass information that is not worth looking at. And Google will respond by giving you a lower rank in the search result list.

- **Give advice that cannot be ignored easily and is readily consumed**

You have done great to this point. Readers are taking a look at what you have to offer because they could not resist your headline and the introduction. But that is not everything. You will want them to come back again when there is something new posted on your blog. That is the point where you want to deliver on your promises. You had them believing in the Promised Land, now take your audience there.

Here are some tips that can help in delivering exceptional solutions and advice to keep your readers coming back for more:

- **Add pit stops in your posts**

Use subheads in your posts to help the readers scan through the post. The article may be long, but the readers are only interested in some parts of it. And that way they will have to browse through to find tea res they want to spend time reading (we all do that).

Another value that subheadings add to the post is by communicating the quality of the content to the readers. If you keep creating irresistible ones, they will have no choice but got through the entire post. And that will lure them back.

Blogging is a battle you have to win, and you can do that by following these tips to draft your subheadings:

- **Create a subtitle after every few paragraphs**

Have as many as you can, depending on the length of your article. They will be used to guide the readers on the route that your post is taking, and they will feel the clarity and ease to follow. It is all about the user experience, and if you can get it right by having them know what every part of the article is about, they will enjoy reading your content for sure.

If the readers do not see any pit stop in the text, they will feel overwhelmed by the post. Think of it as taking a bus for a long trip without any stops or bathroom time. Do you feel the anxiety?

- **Do not make the common subheading mistakes**

Subheadings serve the same purpose as the headings, so you must ensure that you do not make some of the mistakes most bloggers make. When drafting your subheads, ensure that you have skipped these common blunders:

Having plain-label subheadings: one thing you do not want to do at all costs is boring your readers. Labels sometimes become tedious. Your subtitles should be treated like mini headings to invoke more curiosity, not lists to be followed.

Having a spoiler for a subheading: your subheading should not give away too much of what the content is about. The moment your readers know what to expect, they will feel like they already have the summary and will not be compelled to read the text at all.

Having an obscure subheading: whatever you choose to include in the subtitle should not sound too smart. It is not a puzzle for the readers to solve. Most people do not like playing the guessing game. As much as you want them to be curious, clarity is something you must uphold.

For instance, if you are to write about the impact of sleep on anxiety and you decide to have the following as your subheadings:

I.   The essence of good sleep

II.   Reducing stress by creating a functional and steady sleeping routine

III. Do not burn out, catch more Z's

The first subhead is so dull that it feels boring to look at the text that comes under it.

The second one is like the entire text summarized in one sentence — no need to look for more information.

The last subhead does not even make sense.

Those are the three common mistakes you need to avoid when generating subheadings for your text. If done right, a subhead is a sure way to grab the attention of any reader and compel them to have a look at the entire blog content.

- **Compare your subheadings to the main heading of the article**

Everything that falls below a title should communicate the intended message without going off the topic. In other words, your title directs the content of the article towards a common destination. And that means that the subheads should also be in the same line. You do not want to go off track or move away from your main idea. If there is any slight deviation, you need to rethink either the subhead or the heading.

Any sudden twist will leave readers confused and lost along the way. For instance, if your heading is about "How to reduce insulin resistance using a plant-based diet," everything else should point in the same direction. The moment you create a subhead like "Do not let your day job bother you," there is a sudden feeling that everything is twisted here. And the confusion becomes jarring because the two do not seem to relate in whatsoever way. And that might leave your readers feeling like you are not delivering what you promised. The next action would be to press the back button and exit the page altogether.

Maybe you had meant that readers should not let the exhausting practices that happen at work and all the stress get into their way of planning a diet that beats insulin resistance. But the reader who is just scanning the subhead will not understand that, and that is where you get it wrong. You will have created confusion out of something that is valuable and could have helped the readers.

- **Get a format and stick to it in the entire text**

Every writing is done in its unique way, using a style, method, technique, or arrangement that is identifiable with the author and the readers. The moment you go about mixing styles I one text, the whole post will look unpolished and inconsistent. Sometimes the content might be great, but the appeal is not there to be seen.

Readers would like a work that looks nice. It gets them psychologically motivated to read through to the last page. But if the work has inconsistent subheads all through, they may feel bored. You may fail to notice the inconsistency as you write, so it is better to write all the subheads down and go through them once. That way, it is easier to catch if there is something off.

Take a look at these examples:

I.   Have the right physical training routine.

II.   Wake up early for your exercises.

III.   Nothing beats a good sleep.

IV.   Why you should never quit.

V.   How to avoid the slags.

Something feels a bit off reading these subheads back to back. But it is something you may not catch while writing. The first two ones are action plans that you want your readers to have, and the consistency is there to be seen. The third one breaks the flow by changing the style suddenly. And the last two even make it worse as they come in forms of a question and a statement that indicates tips.

- **Unleash the Unexpected**

Readers are always hungry to get the latest trends, updates, and anything new happening around the world. Going for the same old advice and method or writing is not going to cut it. You have to be unique in your way. Become bold and deliver eye-opening solutions. Do what people never expected to be done in that way.

The best way to do that is by listing down your ideas and see if you can add a different touch to each. Give your points a different perspective and tweak them to have unique experiences, something that readers may not be expecting. And that has to do with what you can deliver that other people cannot. Your methods and beliefs should sound different from average and ordinary bloggers.

But you also have to know the limits. Do not go overboard just because you want to add some unique taste or value to your content. The solution you are offering must be as authentic as possible, even if it comes from your perspective. But repeating old tricks does not give you a challenge as a writer. Neither will your readers be impressed. Pour out some espressos to quell their hangover when they least expect it. For instance, you may be writing about blogging, and every blogger has a tip or two about what you are going to say. Make it a bit unique by calling them out of their comfort zone and compete with the top earners in the industry.

- **Follow the same formula**

There is more about methods, and your post should have one. Be it in terms of the relative length of every section or the tone. Something has to stand out as uniform. That is more like following the same style in creating the subheads. There should consistency woven into your blog posts because it gives readers a better experience.

The entire post may be sufficiently uniform that the deviation should be more significant that readers can quickly notice. For instance, if you are talking about tips and the first tip you give has 450 words, you should ensure that all the tips fall in between 550 and 350 words. Otherwise, your text will look sloppy, which might portray a better picture of you as a blogger and a writer.

Such minor mistakes may affect the fluidity of ideas and concepts, and some readers are always susceptible to these details. The best you can do is go through the content and see areas that are a bit off the topic. Alternatively, you can look at three sections: the introduction, any paragraph in the body, and the conclusion and use them to guide your writing formula. An excellent example of a writing method is starting each section with a bold statement, followed by a piece of advice in the middle, then a call to action comes last. That is how you do all the sections of the article. It looks more fluid and highly polished work of art.

- **Be generous with the information at your disposal**

Most bloggers are always afraid to give away too much because they want their readers to sign up for the paid versions and products and therefore end up skimming through their work to offer surface advice. But the fact is, if you are not generous enough, your reads may not see the value of signing up for the paid products. The moment you are giving so much, they will feel compelled to find out more. If the free version is that informative, they will be wondering what you have in store for the paid packages, and that is the impression a beginner should give.

If you have decided to tackle a problem, do not hold back. Work through the issue to the end, dissecting every possible solution and giving great advice. Wow readers with your generosity, and they will be triggered to stick around, building loyalty to your brand.

A post that has a magnitude and wealth of content may be quite an undertaking, but that should not scare you. Go for it, and you will not regret the outcome.

- **Start strong and end in the same way**

The introduction and conclusion are said to be the catchiest parts that should be highly polished. That is quite true, but it does not mean that you ignore the body. By all means, the body is where you intend to offer solutions and deliver on your promises. That means it should also be excellently thought out and put down firmly.

Every section of the post must be great to satisfy readers and give them a better reading experience. You will probably have some strong points than others. Save those for the first two sections and the last one. In between, you can have the other tips filling the body of the blog post. The first ones will grab the attention of the readers, compelling them to dig deep while the last one will give them a feeling of satisfaction, nursing the hangover already created by the average tips in between.

On the other hand, feel your tips are decreasing in value and content; your readers will feel like the post is deflating to the end. And so will their curiosity and the excitement. They should be left feeling pumped by the time they finish reading your posts.

- **Close your post with a bang**

The closing stage is always as important as the starting line. This is where you will want to rally behind the readers and show them how you believe they can do better. This is where you make your readers feel like they can follow the advice and achieve their goals, which are always outlined in the headline of your article. Here is some way that you can close your posts:

- **Deliver a pep talk at the end**

You will want to motivate your readers and show them how hard they have worked and the far they have come. Let them know their capabilities and what to expect once they have implemented the changes and advice offered in the text.

By the time you were struggling with the content, there must have been that inner voice leading as you follow with the writing. That voice that wanted to talk sense into the heads of your readers. Unleash that it at the end. Raise your expectations of them, and they will feel empowered. After all, you don't write to people who cannot take action. They cannot just skim through your blog without doing something positive. Have them take action immediately.

- **Avoid bringing up new information at the end of the text**

This must sound like a common mistake in the blogging business. Where do you get the latest piece of information that you want to add at the conclusion all of a sudden? You had all the time to talk about all the possible solutions and advice that you should not start bringing up something new at the end. Never do that to readers because they will feel ruffled.

When writing a conclusion, try to imagine you are the reader. What would you achieve if you followed your advice, and how would you feel? Home in on their point of view, and you will feel comfortable calling them to action.

- **Have the blog post polished and smoothened in all aspects**

You have finished writing, so what next? Take a break from writing, and possibly have a good rest before you can be back with fresh eyes. Sit down and go through the content as you edit.

This is as essential as any other part of the work you have done. You cannot just post some articles with grammatical errors and typos and expect your readers to be comfortable with that. Some may be okay, but many will take you for an amateur, and readers do not like people who are not sure of what they are doing. Your advice is meant to change someone's life. How would you feel if you are that person, and you learn that the person advising you if not an expert in what he/she is doing? You will exit the page straight away and never come back.

The following checklist should guide your editing:

- Slash all the unnecessary words and phrases. Have only the essential paragraphs that can convey the message you intend to pass.

- Have a motivational tone, not a lecturing one. Anything that sounds like a direct lecture should be twisted to look like a suggestion. Readers feel comfortable with writers that are on their side.

- Add some emotions to the text. Your content should have the right energy. If it sounds boring, nobody will like it.

- Make everything seem appealing and easy on the eye. You should not have paragraphs running long or complex sentences.

- Beak down every complicated word. You can use brackets to clarify what you feel might not be easy to understand.

- Speak in the language that readers are familiar with. You know who you want to address, so it is easier to communicate in their context.

- Remove any idea that is repeated in the text or any contradictory statement.

- Do not backtrack. Ensure all sentences and paragraphs flow smoothly and seamlessly towards the intended direction.

- Avoid having any topic that changes abruptly. Remove any statement that suggests an abrupt turn form the main heading.

- Keep your real style flowing in the text. Do not copy any format that does not come naturally to you. Keep that authentic writing voice.

- Highlight your texts. Use bold letters, italics, and any other style to highlight the areas you feel bear so much weight in the post.

- If there are related points or topics, use bullet and any other numbering format to indicate them.

- Be concrete and specific in what you are addressing. That means that you should not use abstract statements.

- The advice should be concrete and firm. Do not use possibilities as advice.

- Put things in their natural order. For instance, start with the young as you go to the old, small to big, etc.

- Maintain consistency throughout the post. All lists should categorize similar items to ensure you do not have things mixed up in the article.

- Ensure that all essential information is found within the post. Do not be lazy to have external links showing information that you would instead write down as part of the article.

- Eliminate words that look shabby, weak, and flabby. You must also replace passive voice with an active voice where possible.

- Maintain the same rhythm per section of the post. You can adjust the tone as you go down, but no single part should have a different pace.

- Fix all your spelling mistakes, typos, and other grammatical errors.

CHAPTER EIGHT

Creating Lead Magnet Ideas

A lead magnet plays a considerable role in developing customer value optimization system. In definition, a lead magnet is anything valuable that can be exchanged for customers' contact information, especially email addresses. The sole purpose of a lead magnet is to maximize the number of targeted leads you get for every offer you make.

The Importance of Lead Magnet

The best role played by a lead magnet is making the marketing work of a blogger simpler and more manageable. In the early days of blogging, most people would market their sites and posts by asking for subscriptions for newsletters. Nowadays, things have changed.

Even though it involves no money changing hands, having the contacts of your prospects is a valuable tool in your blogging career. It converts the customers into a lead, showing that they are interested in what you have to offer, and allows you to market your services. The problem with the market nowadays is that most people are susceptible and stingy to give their emails, so there must be a catch in for them. That is where lead magnet comes in.

To grab the attention of your readers' persona, you have to give then an irresistible lead magnet, something that can deliver value to them. The moment you get the trust of your leads with free offers, you raise the chances of having them pay for the paid services and also build a positive relationship with them.

Steps to Creating a Lead Magnet

It is always easy to tell if someone puts more effort into their marketing strategy or not. And so, a lead magnet must be directed with a purpose to become active. So the first thing to consider is the persons your lead magnet will serve.

Choose the People You Want to Target

The first market you can make as a blogger is trying to attract everyone to your site using lead magnets. To be effective, you need to be very specific to the kind of people you want your lead magnet to attract. If the people do not feel like the lead magnets meet their wants, they will never take time to download them. Most companies often have multiple buyer personas, but still, you will see every lead magnet targeting only one specific group.

You should not be worried about the people to start attracting because with the time you have lead magnets for every group of readers. What you have to do is picking the group that you feel you can add more value to and then start from there.

Identify the Value Proposition You Want to Offer

Once you have the group you want to focus on, the next step will be getting them something valuable. You must convince them with the offer for them to download your lead magnet. The value of the offer will influence the number of leads your lead magnets attract.

The best offer you can give your readers is something that they need. That would relieve you of the headache of convincing them to download it. Instead of creating something that interests you, identify the needs of the people you have chosen, and try to meet those needs. In that sense, you can offer something small, but it grabs attention than create a large eBook that means less to them.

Going for a common problem is the best way of finding out the desires of the people. You can ask what your readers like and give them just that. Solve their problems better and fast.

Give Your Lead Magnets Identities

At this point, you know your target, and at the same time, you know what to offer them. Giving those lead magnets names will not be hard. The identity should be more appealing and attractive (even more than the offer itself). The same applies to craft a catchy headline for your emails and blog posts, and you should have known why you have to do this at this point.

Choose the Type of Lead Magnets You Want to Offer

You may know what you want to offer your clients, but these things come in different options, and you have to choose the right one. And the type you go for should be able to reflect the value proposition you are making. Here are some tips to help you decide:

Make it simple: a sophisticated lead magnet defeats its purpose. The moment people fail to understand what you are offering them, they will not be convinced to appreciate it. The best way to dot it is by making it as simple as possible, concise, and valuable.

Concentrate on your strong points: what can you offer better? If you a good writer, then you can provide eBooks. If you can take popular pics, then go for that instead.

Prioritize on the in-demand areas: you have to solve immediate problems. Readers will be attracted to your blog if you are offering something that gives them quick solutions. Therefore, you must choose a format that is consumed faster and is highly demanded.

There are many lead magnets that you can choose from. Most of them fall under the following categories:

- Discounts

- Free trials

- Toolkits

- Reports

- Training clips

- Surveys

- Tests

- Sales tools

If you are not sure about the type that can attract your audience, then choose the one that you feel more comfortable about.

Create Your Lead Magnet

All the planning is now behind you, and you have to create the lead magnet. You have to consider all the aspects we have gone through as you create the lead magnets. Remember who you are targeting and what you promised to deliver. You will get things falling in place if you follow all the processes and include the details you have strategized about.

Types of Lead Magnets You Can Offer

Most people think of lead magnets as free eBooks in the form of reports or guides. Those are the most popular ones that bloggers use to get email addresses from their clients. Most customers like them, and they can be related to any niche. However, there are many other types of lead magnets that you can use to generate leads. Below are some examples that you can use to stand out from the crowd.

Reports

This form is by far the simplest and the most used type of lead magnet. That does not make it useful automatically. Most bloggers use them because they work well and can be twisted in any other direction to meet the needs of the people you are focusing on. So, in general, what makes them universal is their specificity. Once directed to focus on the persona of the buyers, they become the go-to thing. The main aim should be to deliver on the promises you made. If that is achieved, your targets will stream to your blog and offer to give you their contact information.

Handouts

Cheat sheets also work well because they can give technical aid that helps your clients to do things faster and save them the complexities. They have a different outlook compared to reports, even though they both come in the form of PDFs.

A handout can be a page or two in length, which means they must be very concise and straight to the point. You have to address the issue straight away and offer immediate solutions quickly, and in a language that is easy to interpret because you will not have the time and space to go around telling stories. In some cases, you can have some images incorporated to give it a better look.

Resource Lists

If targeted for the right people, toolkits can be a great way to offer a lead magnet. You can think of it as a reference to pieces of materials and other resources that you readers can use to solve different problems. This method is usually a way of simplifying their work. You give them what they may get somewhere else but after spending a lot of time researching and sometimes purchasing the materials. For instance, you can offer your readers a time management toolkit.

By this, you will be saving them the time to download or buy such plans.

Video Training

A video is one of the catchiest and engaging formats that you can use as a lead magnet. If you dare to stand in front of a camera and teach someone a skill or two, then this should be a great way of generating leads. Take an example of a podcast. You can offer some motivational talk in areas that people want to listen about, you can demonstrate how to use some home equipment, or you can also show your readers some life hacks that can make their lives simple.

A good example is getting all the transfer rumors from the sporting fraternity if you are blogging about sports, and your audiences like to know what is happening in the transfer market. Then you can host a live webinar and talk about who is joining which club at what price and for how long.

Downloadable Software or Free Trials

Most people are glued to Netflix and have subscribed to the channel for years because of the 30-day free trial they were offered. The best way to get people to know the value of something is by letting them have a taste of it first before they can decide if they want to buy or not. And if the value is up there then you will not have to worry about the purchase, it will come. Many people like to try before they buy.

And you can also make it more effective by not including credit cards because people will not have to worry about canceling their free trials to avoid charges at the end of the trial period.

If you want to give people some software, you can have them download them and install them for free for some time to sample how it all works before they start paying for the services.

Discounts

Everyone likes getting something at a discounted price. And giving up an email address is a smaller price to pay if it means saving some few dollars in buying some essential stuff.

But this is an area that you must be cautious about. If you decide to give people a discount, then ensure that the product you are offering is high on demand. The amount of discount is also something you should consider. If you go for a meager price, you might end up hurting your financial stability. Ata the same time, people will doubt the authenticity of the product if the price is way below the normal, and that can drive them away.

Surveys and Quizzes

To some people, studies have massive value and can be beneficial lead magnets. Okay, before you get this all wrong, it does not take the form of the BuzzFeed quizzes you see on your social media networks. The questions and surveys must be ones that offer real-time solutions to emerging problems. You must touch on areas that affect people, and they feel should be addressed.

You can complete the quizzes by offering some opt-in forms for the readers to finish at the end of the question. This technique will be banking on their participation and anticipation to get some results.

Assessments

An assessment can be similar to a survey but is more specific to a person. For instance, a study can target industry, but an evaluation narrows down to target a firm within that industry. It is more effective for companies that sell their services instead of products.

S0o, in the case of an assessment, the targeted audience will not be looking to get direct answers to their problems but getting an expert opinion about their services. And views can also be used to solve problems.

Sales Tools

Some people are always looking forward to getting pieces of information that can help them make purchasing or selling decisions such as pricing. You can give them some catalogs and other digital sales materials that are more affordable. Anything that can help them make an economical choice can be a god lead magnet that you should use.

In general, whatever you decide to offer in exchange for your readers' emails should be worth their trust. The value pack should be there for them to see and appreciate, and that is the only way that they will comfortable to give away their contact information. And when that is done, ensure that you do not misuse those email addresses by providing what is relevant only.

CHAPTER NINE

Creating Digital Products

They say you will never forget your first digital product as a blogger. And that means selling products online, such as eBooks, courses, or any downloadable version item. Most people feel anxious about what they have created and worry if anybody will like the products, which is very reasonable. When you first see those cash reading in your account, you will feel like someone with a fresh breath of life.

It might not be the first money you make from the blog. However, selling your products to your audience has a different feeling. It changes the entire ballgame, ushering a different level of success. You will feel like all the effort is starting to pay up at last. And that is why you should create a better digital product. The following tips should guide you to have some of the most impressive digital products to sell on your blog.

Set Your Expectations

This is the most important step, no matter how weird it looks. Selling something online to someone you do not know will not be that easy. And that will have to be something you expect. It is crucial to be confident about the knowledge and ideas you want to share with the world.

Some bloggers are selling shabby products, and some make money off it. But they are not the top earners. They do not know how they can turn that knowledge to change people's perspectives. All they care about is the money part of the business. You do not want to join that average group.

You have to bear in mind that everyone has doubts, and it is okay not to be sure about what you are about to do. But sometimes you have to experiment and see if it works out. Otherwise, you will never know what could have been done right. If one product does not sell, try another one. Solicit for feedback from your audience. Let them suggest what they like in the comment section.

Steal ideas from some established bloggers and see if it works well for you. That is probably somewhere you can start from. Best artist steals from each. You just have to ensure that you tweak your version to have an authentic look.

When creating a digital product, keep in mind that people want solutions to their problems. Can you come up with some pill that would let party fanatics get drunk all night without having the adverse side effects that come with excessive drinking? If yes, then you could probably be making $1000 from each pill you sell.

If you can offer real-time solutions to daily problems, people will be willing to pay for the products and pay handsomely. But you will have to deliver on the promises you made because people work so hard for the things they want to buy. And that should be reflected in the value you are creating for them in exchange for their money.

On the contrary, free products or information are never taken seriously, and readers do not put in as much effort on things that are way below the market price. So, you have to know how to value your products if you are to make it big. But that does not mean you cannot offer a discount, as long as it falls within a reasonable range. The moment your products are the cheapest in the market, people will doubt their authenticity.

When you create real solutions to the problems people are facing and sell it, they will thank you for it.

Why Digital Products Are the Best

- The products will not require storage or shipping like physical products, and that saves you some cost and management practices.

- All the profits are mostly yours, and margins are high as long as you have cleared some transaction fees and software costs.

- It is a chance to earn some passive income. Once the systems are automated, you do not even have to manage anything during the selling process. The money just keeps coming in.

- People may love things they can hold (tangible), but digital products offer immediate solutions, and that gives instant gratification that people enjoy.

- The time taken to create or develop a digital product is far less compared to making physical products available for sale.

- In most cases, it is your time that is invested in developing the products. That means that there are fewer costs involved.

These upsides should inspire you to invest more in digital products as they are currently the way to go for bloggers looking to earn extra money.

Build a Good Relationship with Your Audience First

This part is like learning to sell ice to Eskimos. Imagine what you would do if your best friend knocked on your door in the middle of the night and asked for $500, saying it is imperative they have the cash immediately. If you have the money with you would give them without asking questions. That is because you trust them enough to believe whatever reason they have is genuine. The same applies to sales. There must be elements of trust first.

You have to build some trust with your audience, and that is all about sequencing right. The relationship you have with your readers must develop slowly and progress with time. And only after that is done will they trust you with their money. If you are in haste to sell, you might end up losing the readers. But if you wait for the right time to ask, they will gladly support your course and love every bit of it (if you are going to treat them right, of cause).

Generate Better Ideas and Plans

You have earned their trust and are set to have them taste what you have to offer. Now it is time to start doing things. This is the phase where you are required to come up with ideas and plans for implementing your thoughts into finished products.

The first thing to do is to gather information. Go into the market and see what your competitors are doing right (copy that and make it even better) and what they are doing wrong (adjust to beat them). Watch out for what the readers are buying most. Evaluate your ability to provide the products that rea highly demanded. Then lastly, look at what you have at hand.

The moment you have all these sorted out, you will know what is right for your niche, as well as what readers are interested in. That Intel should be enough to help you draw conclusions and get started. The ends are the basis upon which you want to form your hypothesis for the solutions that are needed immediately.

After formulating your proposition, you need to figure out how the solutions look like then draw a strategy that would see you complete the project.

Create an Outline

For a digital product, the framework is usually more detailed and involves many processes than what most people think. It should take the following form at its best:

- A specific and original product name.

- Super headline that complements the name of the product.

- A breakdown of contents into various sections, modules, and lessons.

To ensure that you do this part well, you must ensure that the name of your product is very descriptive and short or straightforward. Your clients should be able to identify and recognize the type of the product by its name alone even if you decide to be a bit cutesy.

In terms of the headline, ensure that it feels like the hook to get readers wanting more. It should address the problem directly or indicate a solution that the product offers. The headline should describe the product thoroughly.

Generally, the outline of your products should include all the information required to develop and sell it. The content must be thorough and well documented.

Put Down your Draft

The best way to eat an elephant is getting a bite at a time. The moment you have laid out an outline of the product, you know how you want it to look like and the solution you want it to offer. What remains is starting the process of developing it. And it has to be done thoughtfully over time until the end.

As much as you do not want the process to drag along for months, you will not also like coming up with a half-baked product. That is why you need multiple drafts to see which one fits into your plans perfectly. The process may be complicated and lengthy, depending on the type of product you are developing. For instance, if it is an eBook, you will have to write all day long for some weeks. If it an online course, then you will have to incorporate some graphics, videos, recordings, as well as some written presentations. And that might take a bit longer than an eBook.

However, regardless of what you are putting your effort into creating, it will always be about the content you are creating, which should be done in phases day by day until the last line is done.

Finalize the Product and Publish It

Once the draft is ready, it is time to sit down and finalize the product as wait for its publication. The first step would be to proofread everything a couple of times and edit the areas you feel should be polished. For an eBook, grammar tools like Grammarly and plagiarism checkers like Turnitin are the best to publish your content. Ensure that it is 100% original and free from any grammatical and spelling mistakes. You can have someone take a look at the product once you are done editing and give you feedback. It is always better to have a third party's approval before you can publish the content

The next step would be figuring out where and how to sell the digital products you have created. There are many platforms you can sell on, such as Teachable, LeadPages, and Clickfunnels (for eBooks, online courses, and any other teaching or revision materials).

Build your sales page, the checkout form, and everything else before posting your product. The procedures are always presented according to the platform you have chosen. After all, this is done. You can act the customer and purchase your product to see how your systems work. You have to ensure that everything is fully functional and that your customers will not be inconvenienced as they try to purchase your products. If it is all systems go, start selling your products.

Learn How to Sell your Products

Well, this is always the hardest part for beginners. All the processes leading to the creation of the product may be a bit longer, but they are the most natural part of the game. Marketing the final product is a different ballgame altogether. It is what determines your success. If you cannot get people to buy, then there is no reason to go through all the processes.

In most cases, people fail not because of the product but their marketing strategy. If you have no idea whatsoever, you will not sell anything, and the effort you put into it will be a waste. The best thing to do is creating sales centered content and channels designed to promote your product.

Create some ads that will give your products an extra push. You can incorporate a video in the product. However, the most important thing to do is having the right product in the right section of the blog post. If the content is talking about healthy diets, you can have your plant-based diet eBook thrown in between the lines as a link. Any other strategy that would help promote your product should be the same as the ones you use to improve your blog content.

The first digital product you sell will always be excellent and inspire you to do more. No matter how long it takes, once you get the first one, the buyers will keep coming (assuming you are offering value for money), and that should give you a way to earn from your blog. Blogging is a battle, anything that happens in between determines if you are going to hang on for ages or get beat and quit within months.

CHAPTER TEN

Affiliate Marketing

Every blogger is supposed to earn a decent income through affiliate marketing, and if that is not the case, then chances are they are not making money to their full potential. These are the added advantages that come with starting a blog, and a blogger must know how to leverage all possible options to get an extra penny.

Affiliate marketing is a promotional program that allows bloggers (who is the affiliate) to receive commissions for the products they advertise on their blogs. For instance, if your blog has an advertisement about a particular product and your reader clicks the link leading to the store and ends up buying that specific good, then the blogger gets paid part of the money as a commission.

Monetizing Your Blog through Affiliate Marketing

While there are millions of blogs around the globe at the moment, in a sense, very few bloggers are making money through their sites. If you are it among the few that are converting their writing into cash, then you need to consider affiliate marketing as a starting point. You can start redirecting readers to products and services and wait to earn commissions every time they make a purchase. It is that simple.

A blog with irresistible will attract many readers, and that will also increase the trust they have for you. When that trust is strong, you can easily convince them to head to other sites and make purchases for some essential materials without compromising the integrity of your blog posts.

Here are some ways in which you can make money on our blog using affiliate marketing:

Go for the Most Relevant Affiliate Programs

The programs only pay per action is taken, which means your readers will not just click the link, and you are paid right away. They have to sign up or buy something for you to get a commission. The chances are that your readers will only follow something relevant and make the desired action. Otherwise, nothing will materialize.

So how do you know the relevant ads for the blog? Ensure that the affiliate program you are joining is closely related to the topic you are focusing on. For instance, if you are talking about photography on your blog, you can apply to become an affiliate for a photo editing tool or camera products and equipment dealer.

The place to join for beginning bloggers is Amazon Associates because it offers various products, and it is easy to find the ones that relate to almost every niche. The commission paid is somewhere between 4% and 15% depending on the products you are promoting and the volume you can move.

Some other targeted affiliate programs are found on clearinghouse websites like Commission Junction, ShareASale, and LinkShare. Some of these and other more are discussed later in this chapter. All the sites looked at in this chapter offer thousands of affiliate programs that any blogger can apply for. You will only be required to sign up for each program separately.

As much you want to go for affiliate programs that are strictly related to your niche to stay relevant, you are not restricted to that alone. You can also go for products that you think may have a positive effect on your audience. Try to figure out what they like. You never know, your photography enthusiast clients might also love video games. What you have to keep in mind is that you do not

96

want to have so many ads on the blog that your readers feel like you are on marketing spree instead of creating blog content to meet their needs.

Use an Affiliate Aggregator Service

This strategy works if your blog topics are diverse. That way, you will need to work with programs like VigLink that have more automated affiliate programs that suit different niches. For instance, if you are discussing a topic on some pairs of shoes found on Zappos, you will not have to sign up with Zappos to promote the product. VigLink automatically appends that affiliate code to your link and pays you the commission you have earned from the sales you improved. The company will, in turn, keep 25% of the commission, but that should not bother you because they negotiate for higher commissions that cover yours too.

VigLink can also go the extra mile and set a new link where there was none instead of just monetizing your links. For instance, if you mention a product on your blog, you will not have to link it to yourself. The program will create the link automatically and pay you whenever there is a sale on the product form the link they created.

The best way to leverage this program is ensuring that your content leans towards commerce and anything business in nature, even though any topic can lead to sales on VigLink.

Create Content that Will Sell

It is common to see bloggers writing content that reviews products because they have affiliate marketing in mind. The ones that earn better are the ones that create content that sell. The power of a blog can easily aggregate loyal readers of specific topics. You can use to make recommendations and provide affiliate links to the suggestions you are talking about.

The moment readers realize you are just throwing links aimlessly, especially if the content itself is below par, they will exit your blog and never come back. You can avoid this by using compelling content to market the products you have chosen to promote. The affiliate ads should be complementing the content and vice versa. Just because you have listed some products do not mean that people will click the links and make purchases. You have to give them something in return. And what a better way than do what you created the blog for in the first place?

Take time to write detailed reviews and only use the affiliate ads to point the information in the right direction.

Carefully Choose Where You Integrate the Affiliate Links

This blunder is probably one that bloggers make. They fail to consider the appropriate places to throw in those affiliate ads. There is a balance between monetization and user experience that should be maintained on a blog. Readers do not visit your website to buy stuff. They want to read your blog posts. You have to ensure that a better part of the post is about what readers want from the weblog. Keep most of the content free from ads. You can have a strategy that works for the audience and your blog. For instance, you can choose up to 10 pages that you want to use for the affiliate promotions. Link the pages form the footer regions, the sidebar, or any place that will give them better visibility without interfering with the content you have written. Alternatively, you can have an ad appearing after every two pages or at the end of the article.

The goal here is not to make money from every page but to ensure that every page can generate money by having ads running from the sides.

Smart affiliate marketing sites and programs for bloggers

Affiliate marketing is an excellent way that a blogger can use to drive income as long as there is good traffic on the blog. For a beginner, you will need to get the right products and platforms. Below are some samples of the affiliate programs you can join:

ShareASale

There are three payment programs offered by ShareASale:

- Pay per sale

- Pay per lead

- Pay per click

The minimum payout you can receive is $50. They have a large market place with many programs that are friendly to bloggers in erns of ease of use. You can check out these affiliate programs from ShareASale:

- An online accounting software called FreshBooks.

- A WordPress hosting engine called WP Engine. For every referral you make to this site, you get paid not less than $200.

- An online photography class that pays from 10% to 25% commission and includes DIY, graphic designs, and many more (CreativeLive).

- A way of creating and printing high-quality photo books and eBooks at a 15% commission (Blurb).

- Blueprint, which is a digital destination that is solely meant for makers. They pay a 4% commission on sales.

- A 7% commission on Snake River Farms (meat selling firm).

- Grammarly, a spelling and grammar checking machine that pays $20 for every sale you make.

- Selling fashion items like jewelry and other accessories online for 12% commission at Stella & Dot.

- Promoting the sales of smart machines used for creating and cutting projects through Cricut at 12% commission.

- Earn 30% commission on sales you promote for a photo editing tool called PicMonkey.

Rakuten (formerly Ebates)

This company offers cashback to some stores for purchases made on their website. The affiliate program is incredible for the additional $25 they give to bloggers for any referral on top of the cashback for purchases. This affiliate program pays out four times every year, and the minimum payout is always $5.01.

HostGator

This tool is a web hosting service provider that offers affordable and user-friendly features. If you refer a customer to their site and the customer ends up signing up for their services, they pay you anywhere between $50 and $125. That means that the more people you send to their sign up website, the more you increase your earnings. For instance, if you refer up to five people in a month, you be paid $50 for every sign-up. If you send between six and ten, you receive $75 per sign up. The amount you earn per sign up continues to rise as you send more people.

The payment method is through PayPal or check. The most impressive thing about it is that there is no minimum payout.

Bluehost

This site is a web hosting service provider, and we have already looked at it earlier in a different capacity. As an affiliate of Bluehost, you can refer people to create accounts on their website, and you will earn $65 for every successful sign-up. To join the program, you will have to click on the affiliate sign up link found on the bottom part of the Bluehost homepage.

Erin Condren

This platform is a platform that offers personalized planners, diaries, journals, notebooks, and other forms of stationeries. For the affiliate program, they offer a 10% commission for every sale made on their merchandise.

The affiliate program also has a 30-day tracking period that allows bloggers to make more money due to the added duration.

CJ Affiliate

One of the largest affiliate markets you will ever come across is the CJ Affiliate. Almost every company has their affiliate programs running on this platform, which makes suitable for nearly all niches. The only problem is that this is not as user-friendly as the other ones on this list. You need to take a lot of time to get familiar with their systems and mode of operations.

With the platform, you get to choose your minimum payout as long as it does not go below $50. The commissions paid out depending on the company you have promoted and the type of products you are marketing.

Ultimate Bundles

This platform offers eBooks and other reading materials at discounted prices. At the same time, they provide affiliate programs that allow bloggers to earn a 40% commission on every bundle that they refer customers to purchase. The topics covered within the packages are mostly lifestyle, such as healthy living, meal planning, etc. and other subjects like blogging, among others.

Amazon

Amazon is by far the most popular affiliate program for both seasoned bloggers and newcomers. The platform is easy to join and has millions of products that you can choose from and advertise on your blog to earn a 10% commission on every successful purchase made. The commission might be small compared to other programs. Still, the most impressive part is that if a customer clicks your link to a product and decides to buy something else on the website instead of the one you are advertising, you still get to earn some commission.

Creative Market

This outlet is an online marketplace that sells digital products, for instance, themes, fonts, graphics, and many other kinds of stuff. It offers a 10% commission for every sale made from a customer you refer to. Additionally, the affiliate program also offers you 10% on all purchases that the same customer makes for the entire year.

Affiliate marketing is one way that bloggers can utilize to add more cash into their baskets. The processes are pretty easy to follow, and you do not have to worry about any maintenance at all. All you need to do is choose a program you think will work for you then convince your readers to buy the products you are advertising. Sit back and wait for the payday.

CHAPTER ELEVEN

Creating a Custom Email

When you have your blog running, you not only have to choose a custom domain name, you also have the opportunity to set up a business (custom) email as well. For instance, is your domain name is MasterStrokes.com, you can also create an account that goes like master@masterstrokes.com or informasterstrokes.com.

What is a Custom Email?

As a blogger, your custom email or a business email is your way of contacting your readers. It is also a marketing tool that will help you promote your blog by sharing your latest blog posts with your subscribers.

An email is always the first thing that your clients should see when correspondence start, which means that it must be ready by the moment you publish your first post. Equally, an email that you are going to use for communication with your readers must be appropriate and straightforward in any way possible. Your email must give a business impression even when it means creating a completely different email address from your old one. It is recommended to have a separate email for the business apart from your personal email. For example, you can have the name of your blog included in the email to make it have that impression to the clients in that regard.

Custom emails are always hosted by specific email holders and come at various ranges in terms of the hosting fee. So it is better to go for a hosting company that does not charge you much for that service. The two best options are Bluehost and Zoho. If you want a custom domain name, then Bluehost is the best, while Zoho is equally essential for people with existing domain names. There are, however, any ways in which you can set up a custom email for your blog.

Why Should You Set Up A Custom Email?

A custom email says a lot about your professionalism and the blog. It is, therefore, very essential that you get an email address that sells your work and builds a reputation for yourself. It will be damaging if you do not come out as a professional because of your choice of an email address.

Additionally, a great email address for the business is a way of getting brand exposure for free.

How You Can Create a Free Custom Email for Your Blog

The following steps are given in the case that you used Bluehost as your host for the blog. If so, then you will have to follow the next steps to have your custom email set up in minutes:

- Once on the homepage (Bluehost), click the Login button found on the upper part of the screen.

- Log into Bluehost by typing in your username and password created at the time of forming your Bluehost account.

- In case you don't know the login password, you can go back to the email sent to you earlier by Bluehost for verification of the account. Alternatively, you can click on the Forgot password tab and follow the link to reset your password.

- Once logged in, click on the email tab that is displayed on the top of the screen and choose the create an email account option.

- Essential in all the details to create an email account then click the create button once done. You have to choose different options that suit you. For instance, you can have unlimited mailbox sizes to ensure that your inbox never gets full.

- Your account is now fully set up. You can log in and start using it immediately.

Anytime you want to log into your email account, you will have to go back to the Bluehost homepage and choose the webmail option displayed on the top right side of the screen.

CHAPTER TWELVE

Promoting your Blog

In the current era, all you need to launch a blog is a few clicks of the mouse, a theme, and words to publish. The barrier to entry is exclusively low, and that not make it a low-value business. If you keep a close eye online, you will realize that there is some fantastic stuff being circulated from time to time.

But it takes more than a mere online presence and engaging blog content to become a successful blogger. You have to get some good traffic coming in to make your other efforts worthwhile. That means you have to promote your blog content to increase visibility, enhance more shares, and build good traffic. Here are some tips for doing just that:

Ensure that You Are a Reliable Source

Anyone can publish some random posts on their blogs and call it a day. But that is not enough to get real traction with the readers you are targeting. To be most successful, you have to stand out by ensuring that what you give your audience is beneficial to them. Before you start hitting the keyboard, you have to evaluate the quality of the content. If you see that it is not helpful enough, then you need to stop and start over.

For content to be helpful, it must add value to the people reading it so that they can see you as a reliable and trustworthy source. If you aim to write something that solves some problems in society, then focus on answering the exact questions and providing better alternatives that can make life easier and sustainable. If you can do that, then odds are you are providing value.

Increase your Chances of Being Found Online

You may be putting so much effort into writing good content for your audience, but if they don't see your posts, then the energy goes to waste. You have to ensure that your blog is quickly found to get your content reaching the people you have targeted. The best way of doing this is by searching for keywords related to your topics and inserting them into your content. This will increase the chances of your blog posts being found in search results

For instance, if you do a google search for "Plant-based diet," you have various articles and blogs popping up at the top of search results. You will find out that the search question matches all the titles of the posts produced as results to the search. That is precisely what you need to be doing to increase your blog content visibility.

Create and Maintain Good Relationships

Anyone that is connected to the blog would not like being used as tools to promote your content unless there is a catch in for them. That means you have to build good relationships with the people you want to connect with as your professional and personal network. You have to engage with everyone directly and contribute to their conversation and personal growth for them to be comfortable, helping you to promote your work. If it is bloggers you want to use to market your work, you have to sell theirs too.

Go to other people's websites and leave positive comments to create a two-way relationship with these people. Add some value to their work and encourage them to share yours in exchange. That would lead to the next point here.

Engage Your Peers and Share their Content

A two-way relationship mentioned above is all about giving something as valuable as what you expect back. It must be an authentic relationship that encourages sharing more information and helping each other out. If it is the attention you can help them with or some real-time solutions, then ensure you provide it entirely.

Please share the content of other bloggers within your niche, and engage in conversations, be it on their blogs or other social media platforms. When you have something new to publish, ask them to take a look at it and give you some feedback. Chances are they will go the extra mile and share your content with their connections.

Join Social Media Networks

The social media platforms you are using to promote your content should not be the only place you share your content. It is recommended to dig deep into forums and community sites and have a decent conversation and share opinions. The more you get involved in these types of conversations, the more trust you build with the people who are capable of sharing your content.

Just ensure that you are engaging your potential audience and not spreading spam. And that means that you are not to share your links in every group you come across. If you want to reach many people with a single post, then you will have to use other tactics. For instance, you can post your article on Facebook and promote it to reach the people that like your page as well as their friends. That would be leveraging the power of social media platforms to boost your content and get outside of your immediate network without being a spammer.

Promote your Content with Email

Email may be dubbed old school since it has been existence for ages, but it is still an effective way of promoting blog content. Get people to opt into your email notifications on your blog and other channels so that you can gather enough addresses to support your work. Increase conversions by offering something in exchange for the email addresses.

Once you have your audience contact information, you can send them your new post or revisit some old contents that are related to the current trending topics of discussion. You can also encourage your subscribers to share your content with other people. If you can have an active call to action to grab the attention of your followers, you have no problem creating traffic to your blog.

Go the Animation Way

Search Engine Land did research that showed how, in 2014, YouTube became the second largest search engine in the world, with billions of visitors watching videos daily. That is evidence enough that people are much attracted to animated content. And that is pretty a right place to cross-promote your content.

So anytime you have a video incorporated in your content, you should know just the right place to have it posted. Be it a presentation or a whiteboard lesson, you can promote your blog by using sites like Vimeo or YouTube. You need to follow the procedures that come with using such sites, such as opening accounts.

Enable Guest Posts

Referral traffic is precious to any blogger out there. And one of the best ways of getting it by guest posting on various blogs within your niche. That way, you be broadening your scope and connecting with influencers and other content producers in the industry. You can offer to contribute on various topics within other people's blogs in exchange for an author box that would enable you to have a link back to your weblog.

You should also provide the same facility for other bloggers to post on your site and have their links on your blog. That strategy would increase the chances for referral traffic on both sites and, at the same time, creates a stable relationship between you and other bloggers within your niche. The plan will also give an added blog content on your blog to fill your blog calendar, which may be the break away from writing that you dearly crave sometimes.

No matter what you have to do, it would help if you took action first to promote your content in any way possible. And that requires a strategic plan and execution. Sit down and set goals you would like to achieve and what you are going to do to get there. Prioritize the things you can get done immediately first before moving to other complex issues that need time.

Be it getting other people to support you or going into it all by yourself; you must make efforts to promote your blog content to get enough traffic that can get you earning decent income off blogging. Put down a plan, then do what you have to do. It is that simple.

Final Word

Blogging is a battle with millions of participants looking to outsmart each other daily. The only way to emerge on top is winning the readers' attention and trust. You have to deliver your ideas in a way that compels the audience to look at your content. But the battle, like any other form of war, is never for the faint-hearted.

Many online distractions will devour your readers and divert their attention, and some of these distractions come from the sites run by your competitors. You have to get the necessary tools to ensure you are not the victim here.

In blogging, there are many learning curves to go through and many installations to do. You will need to sign up for various platforms, employ many social media networks, and market your content and other products to earn extra income. All these require consistency and improvement from your side. Many techniques should be incorporated and styles mastered. At the end of the day what matters is the quality of your work

But all these kinds of stuff do not count if you are going to drown your skills and ideas in amateur writing. If that is the case, then you would better try something else. Readers do not have time for amateurs. So before you start writing, you must ensure you learn how to blog like a pro and master all the tips that will get you paid big. Get the right tools and information, and you will stand out.

Create your blog today and start sharing information; your readers are counting on you!